Harvard
Business
Review

ON

BECOMING A HIGH
PERFORMANCE MANAGER

THE HARVARD BUSINESS REVIEW PAPERBACK SERIES

The series is designed to bring today's managers and professionals the fundamental information they need to stay competitive in a fast-moving world. From the preeminent thinkers whose work has defined an entire field to the rising stars who will redefine the way we think about business, here are the leading minds and landmark ideas that have established the *Harvard Business Review* as required reading for ambitious businesspeople in organizations around the globe.

Other books in the series:

Other books in the series (continued):

Harvard Business Review on Leadership

Harvard Business Review on Managing Diversity

Harvard Business Review on Managing High-Tech Industries

Harvard Business Review on Managing People

Harvard Business Review on Managing Uncertainty

Harvard Business Review on Managing the Value Chain

Harvard Business Review on Managing Your Career

Harvard Business Review on Marketing

Harvard Business Review on Measuring Corporate Performance

Harvard Business Review on Mergers and Acquisitions

Harvard Business Review on Negotiation and Conflict Resolution

Harvard Business Review on Nonprofits

Harvard Business Review on Organizational Learning

Harvard Business Review on Strategic Alliances

Harvard Business Review on Strategies for Growth

Harvard Business Review on Turnarounds

Harvard Business Review on Work and Life Balance

Harvard Business Review

ON

BECOMING A HIGH PERFORMANCE MANAGER

A HARVARD BUSINESS REVIEW PAPERBACK

The *Harvard Business Review* articles in this collection are available as
individual reprints. Discounts apply to quantity purchases. For information and ordering, please contact Customer Service, Harvard Business
School Publishing, Boston, MA 02163. Telephone: (617) 783-7500 or
(800) 988-0886, 8 A.M. to 6 P.M. Eastern Time, Monday through Friday.
Fax: (617) 783-7555, 24 hours a day. E-mail: custserv@hbsp.harvard.edu

Library of Congress Cataloging-in-Publication Data
Harvard business review on becoming a high performance manager.
        p.   cm. — (A Harvard business review paperback)
    Includes index.
    ISBN 1-59139-129-6 (alk. paper)
    1. Executives. 2. Management. I. Harvard Business School Press.
II. Harvard business review. III. Harvard business review paperback
series.
HD38.2 .H3743 2002
658.4´09—dc21   2002012682
                                                         CIP

*The paper used in this publication meets the requirements of the Ameri-
can National Standard for Permanence of Paper for Publications and
Documents in Libraries and Archives Z39.48-1992.*

Contents

Harvard Business Review

ON

BECOMING A HIGH
PERFORMANCE MANAGER

Management Time

Who's Got the Monkey?

WILLIAM ONCKEN, JR., AND
DONALD L. WASS

Executive Summary

MANY MANAGERS FEEL OVERWHELMED. They have
too many problems—too many monkeys—on their backs.
All too often, they say, they find themselves running out of
time while their subordinates are running out of work.
Such is the common phenomenon described by the late
William Oncken, Jr., and Donald L. Wass in this 1974
HBR classic. They tell the engaging story of an overburdened manager who has unwittingly taken on all of his
subordinates' problems.

If, for example, an employee has a problem and the
manager says, "let me think about that and get back to
you," the monkey has just leaped from the subordinate's
back to the manager's. This article describes how the
manager can delegate effectively to keep most monkeys
on the subordinate's back. It offers suggestions on the
care and feeding of monkeys and on how managers
can transfer initiative.

1

In his accompanying commentary, Stephen R. Covey discusses both the enduring power of this message and how theories of time management have progressed beyond these ideas. Management thinkers and executives alike now realize that bosses cannot just give a monkey back to their subordinates. Subordinates must first be empowered, and that's hard and complicated work. It means bosses have to develop their subordinates and establish trust.

Perhaps even more important and relevant than it was 25 years ago, Covey says, this article is a powerful wake-up call for managers at risk for carrying too many monkeys.

WHY IS IT THAT MANAGERS ARE typically running out of time while their subordinates are typically running out of work? Here we shall explore the meaning of management time as it relates to the interaction between managers and their bosses, their peers, and their subordinates.

Specifically, we shall deal with three kinds of management time:

Boss-imposed time—used to accomplish those activities that the boss requires and that the manager cannot disregard without direct and swift penalty.

System-imposed time—used to accommodate requests from peers for active support. Neglecting these requests will also result in penalties, though not always as direct or swift.

Self-imposed time—used to do those things that the manager originates or agrees to do. A certain portion of this kind of time, however, will be taken by subordinates and is called *subordinate-imposed time*. The remaining portion will be the manager's own and is called *discretionary time*. Self-imposed time is not subject to penalty since neither the boss nor the system can discipline the manager for not doing what they didn't know he had intended to do in the first place.

To accommodate those demands, managers need to control the timing and the content of what they do. Since what their bosses and the system impose on them are subject to penalty, managers cannot tamper with those requirements. Thus their self-imposed time becomes their major area of concern.

Managers should try to increase the discretionary component of their self-imposed time by minimizing or doing away with the subordinate component. They will then use the added increment to get better control over their boss-imposed and system-imposed activities. Most managers spend much more time dealing with subordinates' problems than

In accepting the monkey, the manager has voluntarily assumed a position subordinate to his subordinate.

they even faintly realize. Hence we shall use the monkey-on-the-back metaphor to examine how subordinate-imposed time comes into being and what the superior can do about it.

Where Is the Monkey?

Let us imagine that a manager is walking down the hall and that he notices one of his subordinates, Jones, coming his way. When the two meet, Jones greets the manager with, "Good morning. By the way, we've got a problem. You see. . . ." As Jones continues, the manager recognizes in this problem the two characteristics common to all the problems his subordinates gratuitously bring to his attention. Namely, the manager knows (a) enough to get involved, but (b) not enough to make the on-the-spot decision expected of him. Eventually, the manager says, "So glad you brought this up. I'm in a rush right now. Meanwhile, let me think about it, and I'll let you know." Then he and Jones part company.

Let us analyze what just happened. Before the two of them met, on whose back was the "monkey"? The subordinate's. After they parted, on whose back was it? The manager's. Subordinate-imposed time begins the moment a monkey successfully leaps from the back of a subordinate to the back of his or her superior and does not end until the monkey is returned to its proper owner for care and feeding. In accepting the monkey, the manager has voluntarily assumed a position subordinate to his subordinate. That is, he has allowed Jones to make him her subordinate by doing two things a subordinate is generally expected to do for a boss—the manager has accepted a responsibility from his subordinate, and the manager has promised her a progress report.

The subordinate, to make sure the manager does not miss this point, will later stick her head in the manager's office and cheerily query, "How's it coming?" (This is called supervision.)

Or let us imagine in concluding a conference with Johnson, another subordinate, the manager's parting words are, "Fine. Send me a memo on that."

Let us analyze this one. The monkey is now on the subordinate's back because the next move is his, but it is poised for a leap. Watch that monkey. Johnson dutifully writes the requested memo and drops it in his out-basket. Shortly thereafter, the manager plucks it from his in-basket and reads it. Whose move is it now? The manager's. If he does not make that move soon, he will get a follow-up memo from the subordinate. (This is another form of supervision.) The longer the manager delays, the more frustrated the subordinate will become (he'll be spinning his wheels) and the more guilty the manager will feel (his backlog of subordinate-imposed time will be mounting).

Or suppose once again that at a meeting with a third subordinate, Smith, the manager agrees to provide all the necessary backing for a public relations proposal he has just asked Smith to develop. The manager's parting words to her are, "Just let me know how I can help."

Now let us analyze this. Again the monkey is initially on the subordinate's back. But for how long? Smith realizes that she cannot let the manager "know" until her proposal has the manager's approval. And from experience, she also realizes that her proposal will likely be sitting in the manager's briefcase for weeks before he eventually gets to it. Who's really got the monkey? Who will be checking up on whom? Wheel spinning and bottlenecking are well on their way again.

A fourth subordinate, Reed, has just been transferred from another part of the company so that he can launch and eventually manage a newly created business venture. The manager has said they should get together soon to hammer out a set of objectives for the new job, adding, "I will draw up an initial draft for discussion with you."

Let us analyze this one, too. The subordinate has the new job (by formal assignment) and the full responsibility (by formal delegation), but the manager has the next move. Until he makes it, he will have the monkey, and the subordinate will be immobilized.

Why does all of this happen? Because in each instance the manager and the subordinate assume at the outset, wittingly or unwittingly, that the matter under consideration is a joint problem. The monkey in each case begins its career astride both their backs. All it has to do is move the wrong leg, and—presto!—the subordinate deftly disappears. The manager is thus left with another acquisition for his menagerie. Of course, monkeys can be trained not to move the wrong leg. But it is easier to prevent them from straddling backs in the first place.

Who Is Working for Whom?

Let us suppose that these same four subordinates are so thoughtful and considerate of their superior's time that they take pains to allow no more than three monkeys to leap from each of their backs to his in any one day. In a five-day week, the manager will have picked up 60 screaming monkeys—far too many to do anything about them individually. So he spends his subordinate-imposed time juggling his "priorities."

Late Friday afternoon, the manager is in his office with the door closed for privacy so he can contemplate the situation, while his subordinates are waiting outside to get their last chance before the weekend to remind him that he will have to "fish or cut bait." Imagine what they are saying to one another about the manager as they wait: "What a bottleneck. He just can't make up his mind. How anyone ever got that high up in our company without being able to make a decision we'll never know."

The manager can now see, with the clarity of a revelation on a mountaintop, that the more he gets caught up, the more he will fall behind.

Worst of all, the reason the manager cannot make any of these "next moves" is that his time is almost entirely eaten up by meeting his own boss-imposed and system-imposed requirements. To control those tasks, he needs discretionary time that is in turn denied him when he is preoccupied with all these monkeys. The manager is caught in a vicious circle. But time is a-wasting (an understatement). The manager calls his secretary on the intercom and instructs her to tell his subordinates that he won't be able to see them until Monday morning. At 7 p.m., he drives home, intending with firm resolve to return to the office tomorrow to get caught up over the weekend. He returns bright and early the next day only to see, on the nearest green of the golf course across from his office window, a foursome. Guess who?

That does it. He now knows who is really working for whom. Moreover, he now sees that if he actually accomplishes during this weekend what he came to accomplish, his subordinates' morale will go up so sharply that they will each raise the limit on the number of monkeys they will let jump from their backs to his. In short, he now sees, with the clarity of a revelation on a mountaintop, that the more he gets caught up, the more he will fall behind.

He leaves the office with the speed of a person running away from a plague. His plan? To get caught up on something else he hasn't had time for in years: a weekend with his family. (This is one of the many varieties of discretionary time.)

Sunday night he enjoys ten hours of sweet, untroubled slumber, because he has clear-cut plans for Monday. He is going to get rid of his subordinate-imposed time. In exchange, he will get an equal amount of discretionary time, part of which he will spend with his subordinates to make sure that they learn the difficult but rewarding managerial art called "The Care and Feeding of Monkeys."

The manager will also have plenty of discretionary time left over for getting control of the timing and the content not only of his boss-imposed time but also of his system-imposed time. It may take months, but compared with the way things have been, the rewards will be enormous. His ultimate objective is to manage his time.

Getting Rid of the Monkeys

The manager returns to the office Monday morning just late enough so that his four subordinates have collected outside his office waiting to see him about their monkeys. He calls them in one by one. The purpose of each interview is to take a monkey, place it on the desk between them, and figure out together how the next move might conceivably be the subordinate's. For certain monkeys, that will take some doing. The subordinate's next move may be so elusive that the manager may decide—just for now—merely to let the monkey sleep on the subordinate's back overnight and have him or her return with it at an appointed time the next morning to continue the joint quest for a more substantive move by the subordinate. (Monkeys sleep just as soundly overnight on subordinates' backs as they do on superiors'.)

As each subordinate leaves the office, the manager is rewarded by the sight of a monkey leaving his office on the subordinate's back. For the next 24 hours, the subordinate will not be waiting for the manager; instead, the manager will be waiting for the subordinate.

Later, as if to remind himself that there is no law against his engaging in a constructive exercise in the interim, the manager strolls by the subordinate's office, sticks his head in the door, and cheerily asks, "How's it coming?" (The time consumed in doing this is discretionary for the manager and boss imposed for the subordinate.)

When the subordinate (with the monkey on his or her back) and the manager meet at the appointed hour the next day, the manager explains the ground rules in words to this effect:

"At no time while I am helping you with this or any other problem will your problem become my problem. The instant your problem becomes mine, you no longer have a problem. I cannot help a person who hasn't got a problem.

"When this meeting is over, the problem will leave this office exactly the way it came in—on your back. You may ask my help at any appointed time, and we will make a joint determination of what the next move will be and which of us will make it.

"In those rare instances where the next move turns out to be mine, you and I will determine it together. I will not make any move alone."

The manager follows this same line of thought with each subordinate until about 11 A.M., when he realizes that he doesn't have to close his door. His monkeys are gone. They will return—but by appointment only. His calendar will assure this.

Transferring the Initiative

What we have been driving at in this monkey-on-the-back analogy is that managers can transfer initiative back to their subordinates and keep it there. We have tried to highlight a truism as obvious as it is subtle:

namely, before developing initiative in subordinates, the manager must see to it that they *have* the initiative. Once the manager takes it back, he will no longer have it and he can kiss his discretionary time good-bye. It will all revert to subordinate-imposed time.

Nor can the manager and the subordinate effectively have the same initiative at the same time. The opener, "Boss, we've got a problem," implies this duality and represents, as noted earlier, a monkey astride two backs, which is a very bad way to start a monkey on its career. Let us, therefore, take a few moments to examine what we call "The Anatomy of Managerial Initiative."

There are five degrees of initiative that the manager can exercise in relation to the boss and to the system:

1. wait until told (lowest initiative);

2. ask what to do;

3. recommend, then take resulting action;

4. act, but advise at once;

5. and act on own, then routinely report (highest initiative).

Clearly, the manager should be professional enough not to indulge in initiatives 1 and 2 in relation either to the boss or to the system. A manager who uses initiative 1 has no control over either the timing or the content of boss-imposed or system-imposed time and thereby forfeits any right to complain about what he or she is told to do or when. The manager who uses initiative 2 has control over the timing but not over the content. Initiatives 3, 4, and 5 leave the manager in control of both, with the greatest amount of control being exercised at level 5.

In relation to subordinates, the manager's job is twofold. First, to outlaw the use of initiatives 1 and 2, thus giving subordinates no choice but to learn and master "Completed Staff Work." Second, to see that for each problem leaving his or her office there is an agreed-upon level of initiative assigned to it, in addition to an agreed-upon time and place for the next manager-subordinate conference. The latter should be duly noted on the manager's calendar.

The Care and Feeding of Monkeys

To further clarify our analogy between the monkey on the back and the processes of assigning and controlling, we shall refer briefly to the manager's appointment schedule, which calls for five hard-and-fast rules governing the "Care and Feeding of Monkeys." (Violation of these rules will cost discretionary time.)

Rule 1. Monkeys should be fed or shot. Otherwise, they will starve to death, and the manager will waste valuable time on postmortems or attempted resurrections.

Rule 2. The monkey population should be kept below the maximum number the manager has time to feed. Subordinates will find time to work as many monkeys as he or she finds time to feed, but no more. It shouldn't take more than five to 15 minutes to feed a properly maintained monkey.

Rule 3. Monkeys should be fed by appointment only. The manager should not have to hunt down starving monkeys and feed them on a catch-as-catch-can basis.

Rule 4. Monkeys should be fed face-to-face or by telephone, but never by mail. (Remember—with mail, the next move will be the manager's.) Documentation may add to the feeding process, but it cannot take the place of feeding.

Rule 5. Every monkey should have an assigned next feeding time and degree of initiative. These may be revised at any time by mutual consent but never allowed to become vague or indefinite. Otherwise, the monkey will either starve to death or wind up on the manager's back.

"GET CONTROL OVER the timing and content of what you do" is appropriate advice for managing time. The first order of business is for the manager to enlarge his or her discretionary time by eliminating subordinate-imposed time. The second is for the manager to use a portion of this newfound discretionary time to see to it that each subordinate actually has the initiative and applies it. The third is for the manager to use another portion of the increased discretionary time to get and keep control of the timing and content of both boss-imposed and system-imposed time. All these steps will increase the manager's leverage and enable the value of each hour spent in managing management time to multiply without theoretical limit.

Making Time for Gorillas

Stephen R. Covey

WHEN BILL ONCKEN WROTE this article in 1974, managers were in a terrible bind. They were desperate for a way to free up their time, but command and control was the status quo. Managers felt they weren't allowed to empower their subordinates to make decisions. Too dangerous. Too risky. That's why Oncken's message—give the monkey back to its rightful owner—involved a critically important paradigm shift. Many managers working today owe him a debt of gratitude.

It is something of an understatement, however, to observe that much has changed since Oncken's radical recommendation. Command and control as a management philosophy is all but dead, and "empowerment" is the word of the day in most organizations trying to thrive in global, intensely competitive markets. But command and control stubbornly remains a common practice. Management thinkers and executives have discovered in the last decade that bosses cannot just give a monkey back to their subordinates and then merrily get on with their own business. Empowering subordinates is hard and complicated work.

The reason: when you give problems back to subordinates to solve themselves, you have to be sure that they have both the desire and the ability to do so. As every executive knows, that isn't always the case. Enter a whole new set of problems. Empowerment often means you have to develop people, which is initially much more time consuming than solving the problem on your own.

Just as important, empowerment can only thrive when the whole organization buys into it—when formal systems and the informal culture support it. Managers need to be rewarded for delegating decisions and developing people. Otherwise, the degree of real empowerment in an organization will vary according to the beliefs and practices of individual managers.

But perhaps the most important lesson about empowerment is that effective delegation—the kind Oncken advocated—depends on a trusting relationship between a manager and his subordinate. Oncken's message may have been ahead of his time, but what he suggested was still a fairly dictatorial solution. He basically told bosses, "Give the problem back!" Today, we know that this approach by itself is too authoritarian. To delegate effectively, executives need to establish a running dialogue with subordinates. They need to establish a partnership. After all, if subordinates are afraid of failing in front of their boss, they'll keep coming back for help rather than truly take initiative.

Oncken's article also doesn't address an aspect of delegation that has greatly interested me during the past two decades—that many managers are actually *eager* to take on their subordinates' monkeys. Nearly all the managers I talk with agree that their people are underutilized in their present jobs. But even some of the most successful, seemingly self-assured executives have talked about how hard it is to give up control to their subordinates.

I've come to attribute that eagerness for control to a common, deep-seated belief that rewards in life are scarce and fragile. Whether they learn it from their family, school, or athletics, many people establish an identity by comparing themselves with others. When they see others gain power, information, money, or recognition, for instance, they experience what the psychologist Abraham Maslow called "a feeling of deficiency"—a sense that something is being taken from them. That makes it hard for them to be genuinely happy about the success of others—even of their loved ones. Oncken implies that managers can easily give back or refuse monkeys, but many managers may subconsciously fear that a subordinate taking the initiative will make them appear a little less strong and a little more vulnerable.

How, then, do managers develop the inward security, the mentality of "abundance," that would enable them to relinquish control and seek the growth and development of those around them? The work I've done with numerous organizations suggests that managers who live with integrity according to a principle-based value system are most likely to sustain an empowering style of leadership.

Given the times in which he wrote, it was no wonder that Oncken's message resonated with managers. But it was reinforced by Oncken's wonderful gift for storytelling. I got to know Oncken on the speaker's circuit in the 1970s, and I was always impressed by how he dramatized his ideas in colorful detail. Like the Dilbert comic strip, Oncken had a tongue-in-cheek style that got to the core of managers' frustrations and made them want to take back control of their time. And the monkey on your back wasn't just a metaphor for Oncken—it was his personal symbol. I saw him several times walking through airports with a stuffed monkey on his shoulder.

I'm not surprised that his article is one of the two best-selling HBR articles ever. Even with all we know about empowerment, its vivid message is even more important and relevant now than it was 25 years ago. Indeed, Oncken's insight is a basis for my own work on time management, in which I have people categorize their activities according to urgency and importance. I've heard from executives again and again that half or more of their time is spent on matters that are urgent but not important. They're trapped in an endless cycle of dealing with other people's monkeys, yet they're reluctant to help those people take their own initiative. As a result, they're often too busy to spend the time they need on the real gorillas in their organization. Oncken's article remains a powerful wake-up call for managers who need to delegate effectively.

Originally published in November–December 1999
Reprint 99609

Beware the Busy Manager

HEIKE BRUCH AND SUMANTRA GHOSHAL

Executive Summary

MANAGERS WILL TELL YOU THAT the resource they
lack most is time. If you watch them, you'll see them rush-
ing from meeting to meeting, checking their e-mail constantly, fighting fires—an astonishing amount of fast-
moving activity that allows almost no time for reflection.
Managers think they are attending to important matters,
but they're really just spinning their wheels.

For the past ten years, the authors have studied the
behavior of busy managers, and their findings should
frighten you: Fully 90% of managers squander their time
in all sorts of ineffective activities. A mere 10% of managers spend their time in a committed, purposeful, and
reflective manner.

Effective action relies on a combination of two traits:
focus—the ability to zero in on a goal and see the task
through to completion—and *energy*—the vigor that comes

from intense personal commitment. Focus without energy devolves into listless execution or leads to burnout. Energy without focus dissipates into aimless busyness or wasteful failures. Plotting these two traits into a matrix provides a useful framework for understanding productivity levels of different managers.

Managers who suffer from low levels of both energy and focus are the procrastinators: they dutifully perform routine tasks but fail to take initiative. Disengaged managers have high focus but low energy: They have reservations about the jobs they are asked to do, so they approach them halfheartedly. Distracted managers have high energy but low focus: they confuse frenetic activity with constructive action. Purposeful managers are both highly energetic and highly focused: These are the managers who accomplish the most.

This article will help you identify which managers in your organization are making a real difference—and which just look busy.

If you listen to executives, they'll tell you that the resource they lack most is time. Every minute is spent grappling with strategic issues, focusing on cost reduction, devising creative approaches to new markets, beating new competitors. But if you watch them, here's what you'll see: They rush from meeting to meeting, check their e-mail constantly, extinguish fire after fire, and make countless phone calls. In short, you'll see an astonishing amount of fast-moving activity that allows almost no time for reflection.

No doubt, executives are under incredible pressure to perform, and they have far too much to do, even when they work 12-hour days. But the fact is, very few managers use their time as effectively as they could. They think they're attending to pressing matters, but they're really just spinning their wheels.

The awareness that unproductive busyness—what we call "active non-action"—is a hazard for managers is not new. Managers themselves bemoan the problem, and researchers such as Jeffrey Pfeffer and Robert Sutton have examined it (see "The Smart-Talk Trap," HBR May–June 1999). But the underlying dynamics of the behavior are less well understood.

For the past ten years, we have studied the behavior of busy managers in nearly a dozen large companies, including Sony, LG Electronics, and Lufthansa. The managers at Lufthansa were especially interesting to us because in the last decade, the company underwent a complete transformation—from teetering on the brink of bankruptcy in the early 1990s to earning a record profit of DM 2.5 billion in 2000, thanks in part to the leadership of its managers. We interviewed and observed some 200 managers at Lufthansa, each of whom was involved in at least one of the 130 projects launched to restore the company's exalted status as one of Europe's business icons.

Our findings on managerial behavior should frighten you: Fully 90% of managers squander their time in all sorts of ineffective activities. In other words, a mere 10% of managers spend their time in a committed, purposeful, and reflective manner. This article will help you identify which managers in your organization are making a real difference and which just look or sound busy. Moreover, it will show you how to improve the effectiveness of all your managers—and maybe even your own.

Focus and Energy

Managers are not paid to make the inevitable happen. In most organizations, the ordinary routines of business chug along without much managerial oversight. The job of managers, therefore, is to make the business do more than chug—to move it forward in innovative, surprising ways. After observing scores of managers for many years, we came to the conclusion that managers who take effective action (those who make difficult—even seemingly impossible—things happen) rely on a combination of two traits: focus and energy.

Think of *focus* as concentrated attention—the ability to zero in on a goal and see the task through to completion. Focused managers aren't in reactive mode; they choose not to respond immediately to every issue that comes their way or get sidetracked from their goals by distractions like e-mail, meetings, setbacks, and unforeseen demands. Because they have a clear understanding of what they want to accomplish, they carefully weigh their options before selecting a course of action. Moreover, because they commit to only one or two key projects, they can devote their full attention to the projects they believe in.

Consider the steely focus of Thomas Sattelberger, currently Lufthansa's executive vice president, product and service. In the late 1980s, he was convinced that a corporate university would be an invaluable asset to a company. He believed managers would enroll to learn how to challenge old paradigms and to breathe new life into the company's operational practices, but his previous employer balked at the idea. After joining Lufthansa, Sattelberger again prepared a detailed business case that carefully aligned the goals of the university with the company's larger organizational agenda. When he made his proposal to the executive board, he was met with strong skepticism: Many believed Lufthansa would be better served by focusing on cutting costs and improving processes. But he kept at it for another four years, chipping away at the objections. In 1998, Lufthansa School of Business became the first corporate university in Germany—and a change engine for Lufthansa.

Think of the second characteristic—*energy*—as the vigor that is fueled by intense personal commitment. Energy is what pushes managers to go the extra mile when tackling heavy workloads and meeting tight deadlines. The team that created the Sony Vaio computer—the first PC to let users combine other Sony technologies, such as digital cameras, portable music players, and camcorders—showed a lot of energy. Responding to CEO Nobuyuki Idei's challenge to create an integrated technological playground for a burgeoning generation of "digital dream kids," Hiroshi Nakagawa and his team put in 100-hour weeks to create the kind of breakthrough product Idei hoped for. One manager, Kazumasa Sato, was so devoted to the project that he spent every weekend for three years conducting consumer reconnaissance in electronics shops. Sato's research into consumer buying patterns helped Sony develop a shop layout that enhanced traffic flow and, by extension, sales. In the end, the Vaio captured a significant share of the Japanese PC market.

While both focus and energy are positive traits, neither alone is sufficient to produce the kind of purposeful action organizations need most from their managers. Focus without energy devolves into listless execution or leads to burnout. Energy without focus dissipates into purposeless busyness or, in its most destructive form, a series of wasteful failures. We found that plotting the two characteristics in a matrix offered a useful framework for diagnosing the causes of nonproductive activity as well as the sources of purposeful action. The exhibit "The Focus–Energy Matrix" identifies four types of behavior: disengagement, procrastination, distraction, and purposefulness.

Before we look at each type more closely, we should note that these behaviors have both internal and external causes. Some people are born with high levels of energy, for example, and some, by nature, are more self-reflective. But it is important not to overlook the organizational context of these behaviors. Some companies foster fire-fighting cultures; others breed cynicism and,

The Focus–Energy Matrix

A mere 10% of managers are purposeful—that is, both highly energetic and highly focused. They use their time effectively by carefully choosing goals and then taking deliberate actions to reach them. Managers that fall into the other groups, by contrast, are usually just spinning their wheels; some procrastinate, others feel no emotional connection to their work, and still others are easily distracted from the task at hand. Although they look busy, they lack either the focus or the energy required for making any sort of meaningful change.

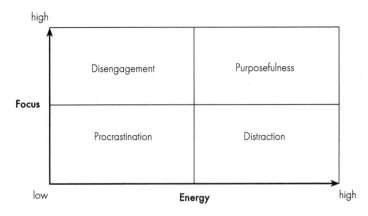

hence, low levels of commitment in their workers. To change the behaviors of your managers, it may be necessary to alter the organizational landscape.

The Procrastinators

Of the managers we studied, some 30% suffered from low levels of both energy and focus; we call these managers the procrastinators. Although they dutifully perform routine tasks—attending meetings, writing memos, making phone calls, and so on—they fail to take initiative, raise the level of performance, or engage with strategy.

Some procrastinators hesitate, Hamlet-like, until the window of opportunity for a project has closed. At Lufthansa, for instance, the manager who was charged with developing an internal survey delayed beginning the project until the deadline passed. "I could have done [the work]," he admits, "but for some reason, I could not get started." The nearer the deadline loomed, the more he busied himself on other projects, rationalizing that he couldn't turn to this task until he cleared his desk of less important jobs.

People often procrastinate when they feel insecure or fear failure. One young lawyer, assigned a key role in an important merger project, was initially excited about the prospect of making a presentation to the executive board. But as time passed, he found the challenge of the task overwhelming. He began imagining horrible scenarios: losing his train of thought, saying the wrong thing, seeing the stifled yawns and suppressed smirks of his audience. He became so obsessed with the notion of failure that he was almost paralyzed.

Other procrastinators coast along in the chronically passive state that psychologist Martin Seligman called "learned helplessness." At some point in their lives, they were punished or suffered negative consequences when they took initiative. Now, as managers, they believe that any effort they make will be shot down. They think they have no control over events, so they do nothing, which can ultimately debilitate their companies.

Surprisingly, in the early phases of Lufthansa's turnaround—when things were chaotic and managerial jobs were relatively unstructured—fewer managers than we expected were procrastinators. But when circumstances returned to normal and formal procedures were reestablished, many managers lost both focus and energy. They stopped setting goals for themselves and became passive. This reinforced our sense that procrastination doesn't wholly depend on personality; it can be influenced by organizational factors.

The Disengaged

Roughly 20% of managers fall into the disengaged category; they exhibit high focus but have low levels of energy. Some of these managers are simply exhausted and lack the inner resources to reenergize themselves. Others feel unable to commit to tasks that hold little meaning for them. Disengaged managers have strong reservations about the jobs they are asked to do; as a result, they approach them halfheartedly.

Many managers in this group practice a form of denial we call "defensive avoidance": Rather than acknowledging a problem and taking steps to correct it, they convince themselves that the problem doesn't exist. Plenty of denial was at play when Lufthansa stood at the brink of bankruptcy in 1992. Even though the entire industry faced a severe downturn and Lufthansa was losing revenue, these managers ignored or reinterpreted market signals, convincing themselves that the company's expansionist strategy was correct. Many of them continued to hire new employees in the face of massive operating losses.

By contrast, some disengaged managers refuse to take action—even when it's obviously needed. One manager responsible for ground services in a major airport, for example, fully understood the threat of bankruptcy and the need to make radical changes. He enthusiastically participated in all the change management meetings and offered ideas for improving operational productivity. Yet deep down, he believed his job was to protect his area and his people. He convinced himself that his department was a core group and should be spared from layoffs. Later, when it become clear that cuts in all areas were inevitable, he agreed to the layoffs in principle, but his personal discomfort kept him from truly committing to them. He delayed making the decision and invested little energy in making the right cuts. As a consequence, his results were less than stellar.

Disengaged managers tend to be extremely tense. That's hardly surprising, for they are often plagued by feelings of anxiety, uncertainty, anger, frustration, and alienation. They deal with those emotions by withdrawing and doing the bare minimum, which make the situations worse. Despite their low levels of energy, these managers suffer from burnout far more frequently than their colleagues do. And they are easily overwhelmed by unexpected events.

While some managers are inherently more likely than others to distance themselves from their work, disengagement is often a result of organizational processes. In a major U.S. oil company, for example, we witnessed a committed and enthusiastic manager gradually become apathetic. An IT specialist, he was assigned to an interdisciplinary strategy-development task force that was charged with creating a new business model for an

Distracted managers feel a desperate need to do something—anything. This makes them as dangerous as the proverbial bull in a china shop.

upstream division. The team came up with several radical proposals, but they were met with lukewarm responses from senior managers. After several months, the team's ideas were diluted to the point that not even the IT manager found them interesting. What had once been an exciting task became a farce, from his point of view. Believing that no one was interested in new ideas, he concluded that he was foolish to have been as engaged as he was. "I distanced myself," he says. "I knew that none of our innovative ideas would ever make it to implementation. So I continued working out concepts and ideas—but with no skin in the game."

To be fair, even the best organizations occasionally create cynics out of enthusiasts. But some organizations seem to make a practice of it by consistently sabotaging any flickers of creativity or initiative.

The Distracted

By far the largest group of managers we studied—more than 40%—fall into the distracted quadrant: those well-intentioned, highly energetic but unfocused people who confuse frenetic motion with constructive action. When they're under pressure, distracted managers feel a desperate need to do something—anything. That makes them as dangerous as the proverbial bull in a china shop.

In 1992, for example, when Lufthansa's senior management made it clear that the company was going to have to reduce expenses, managers in this category shot first and aimed later. "Everybody knew that we had to do everything to reduce costs, and I was frantic," admits one. "I let go of people who were vital to our future. We had to re-recruit them and hire them back later at higher salaries." He had acted too quickly because he felt that something had to happen fast. He didn't take the time to consider what, exactly, that "something" should be.

Because they don't stop to reflect, distracted managers tend to have trouble developing strategies and adjusting their behaviors to new requirements. One manager on the task force charged with driving Lufthansa's change strategy assigned responsibilities according to functional categories instead of deliberately choosing the best person for each job. "We made the technical guy responsible for technical issues and the marketing guy for marketing issues," he says. "You do so many things just because you are used to doing them." He later realized that if he had been less bound by traditional functional silos, the work would have progressed much faster.

Moreover, because distracted managers tend to be shortsighted, they often find themselves over committed. They get involved in multiple projects with the best of intentions, but eventually their interest pales, and they wind up either constantly fighting fires or abandoning the projects altogether. In the space of two months, one HR executive we observed enthusiastically took on three enormous projects—redefining the role of the HR department, renewing the 360-degree feedback system, and creating a leadership development program—over and above his everyday job requirements. In the end, he abandoned one project, passed on responsibility for another, and did a poor job on the third.

Managers are more likely to feel distracted during a crisis, but the behavior is by no means limited to turbulent times. Even in stable business situations, many managers feel enormous pressure to be busy. Of course, some of this pressure is internal: Many insecure managers try to impress others with how much work they have. But the pressure to perform can be amplified by organizations themselves. Indeed, many companies encourage, and even reward, frantic activity. We have noticed, for example, that in organizations whose CEOs and senior executives exhibit aggressive, unreflective behavior, it's far more likely that other managers will be distracted.

The Purposeful

The smallest proportion of managers we studied— around 10%—were both highly energetic and highly focused. Not only do such managers put in more effort than their counterparts, but they also achieve critical, long-term goals more often. Purposeful managers tend to be more self-aware than most people. Their clarity about their intentions, in combination with strong willpower, seems to help them make sound decisions about how to spend their time. They pick their goals—and their battles—with far more care than other managers do.

Making deliberate choices can be a hard and sometimes painful process. Consider the plight of one middle manager at Lufthansa. He had been offered the difficult job of assuring the implementation of 130 do-or-die operations projects that would be overseen by managers more senior than he was. If he failed, a board member told him, he'd probably have to leave the company because he would have upset so many people during the turnaround effort. "I really struggled for a couple of days," he says. Making this huge decision was this manager's personal Rubicon: "After I went through that process, I was sure I really wanted to do it." Lufthansa's successful turnaround was a testament to his conviction.

A sense of personal responsibility for the company's fate also contributes to purposefulness. Convinced that the organization needs them, purposeful managers feel accountable for making a meaningful contribution.

One reason that purposeful managers are so effective is that they are adept at husbanding energy.

"When nobody is responsible, I am responsible," one Lufthansa manager says. "I own an issue and do what I think is necessary—unless and until [CEO] Jürgen Weber pulls me back." Interestingly, many Lufthansa managers refer to their contributions to the turnaround in the stark vocabulary of life and death. Like warriors, they were "fighting for survival," "stanching the loss of blood," or providing "first aid" to the corporate body.

While one could infer that managers become purposeful only when faced with a crisis, the managers we studied did not lose their energy or focus once the turbulence had passed. Rather, they continued to welcome opportunities and pursue new goals. Even after the success of the turnaround was reported in the press and people were ready to celebrate Lufthansa's victory, one purposeful manager, for example, led a wide-ranging cost-management program. By watching costs, he believed, Lufthansa would not merely survive, but thrive.

One reason that purposeful managers are so effective is that they are adept at husbanding energy. Aware of the value of time, they manage it carefully. Some refuse to respond to e-mails, phone calls, or visitors outside certain periods of the day. Others build "think time" into their schedules. One executive, for example, frequently arrived at the office at 6:00 A.M. to ponder issues before his colleagues showed up. "In the busiest times, I slow down and take time off to reflect on what I actually want to achieve and sort what's important from irrelevant noise," he says. "Then I focus on doing what is most important."

Purposeful managers are also skilled at finding ways to reduce stress and refuel. They commonly draw on what we call a "personal well"—a defined source for positive energy. Some work out at the gym or get involved in sports. Others share their fears, frustrations, and thoughts about work with a partner, friend, or colleague. Still others refuel their inner reserves through hobbies like gardening.

Perhaps the biggest difference between purposeful managers and the other types is the way they approach work. Other managers feel constrained by outside forces: their bosses, their peers, their salaries, their job descriptions. They take all those factors into account when they're deciding what's feasible and what isn't. In other words, they work from the outside in. Purposeful managers do the opposite. They decide first what they must achieve and then work to manage the external environment—tapping into resources, building networks, honing skills, broadening their influence—so that, in the end, they meet their goals. A sense of personal volition—the refusal to let other people or organizational constraints set the agenda—is perhaps the subtlest and most important distinction between this group of managers and all the rest.

Indeed, this sense of volition allows purposeful managers to control the external environment. A major drain on most managers' energy is the perception that they have limited influence. Purposeful managers, by contrast, are acutely aware of the choices they can make—and they systematically extend their freedom to act. They manage their bosses' expectations, find ways to independently access required resources, develop relationships with influential people, and build specific competencies that broaden their choices and ability to act.

That's why purposeful managers can place long-term bets and follow through on them. Consider the accomplishments of one of Lufthansa's purposeful managers. During the turnaround, he was responsible for negotiating the tricky relationship between the corporation and the German airline industry's demanding labor unions.

"If you want to build a ship, don't drum up the men to go to the forest to gather wood, saw it, and nail the planks together. Instead, teach them the desire for the sea."

–Antoine de Saint-Exupéry

To develop the trust required to make the tough change agenda work, he initiated a series of meetings between board members and union leaders. Every two weeks, representatives from each wary camp met for three hours and discussed the critical turnaround steps. The board members had reservations because the meetings ate up their time—the one thing they didn't have during this phase. They complained that the meetings weren't producing immediate results—neither cost reductions nor revenue increases. But the executive convinced the board members that a focus on short-term performance would not get them very far in building trusting relationships with union members, which would be essential if they were to turn Lufthansa around. "I told them that we could not hope to transform [Lufthansa] without the help of the employees and that it made no sense to try to hurry trust building," he explains. Over time, the two sides came to trust each other and to reach an extraordinarily high level of consensus. Not only did the company avoid a strike, but the wage concessions achieved in agreement with the union were unique in German history.

Challenge and Choice

We can imagine readers wincing as they ask themselves, "Are only 10% of the managers in my company truly effective?" The number may be higher in your company, but probably not by much. Senior managers can raise the energy and focus levels of their teams—of that we have no doubt. However, trying to prevent managers from losing energy or focus (or both) is an ambitious proposition. It involves paying far more attention to how individual managers perceive the broad meaning of their work, what challenges they face, and the degree of autonomy they enjoy. It can't be done by pulling small-scale HR levers; it can only happen with vision, oversight, and commitment from the top.

In a striking metaphor, the French World War II pilot and writer Antoine de Saint-Exupéry pointed executives in the right direction: "If you want to build a ship, don't drum up the men to go to the forest to gather wood, saw it, and nail the planks together. Instead, teach them the desire for the sea." In managers, a desire for the sea springs from two sources: meaningful challenge and personal choice. If you combine challenge and choice with a sense of profound urgency, you've gone a long way toward creating a recipe for success. Consider the starting point for Lufthansa's turnaround. On a weekend in June 1992, CEO Weber invited about 20 senior managers, as well as the entire executive board, to the company's training center. He wanted to create a network of managers who would drive the change process throughout the company. At the meeting, he revealed the unvarnished facts: Lufthansa was facing a massive shortfall. It was obvious that if things didn't change, the company would be in financial ruin. Weber made it very clear that he didn't have the solution. He gave the managers three days to develop ways to save Lufthansa. If they determined that it could not be saved, he would accept their conclusion, and bankruptcy was assured. Then he and the executive board left.

According to personal accounts of what followed, the place was in chaos for a short time. The managers were shocked at how dire the situation was, and they quickly experienced waves of paralysis, denial, and finger-pointing. But soon they settled down to the problem at hand, and it quickly became clear that they all thought Lufthansa was worth fighting for. Once that fact was established, a kind of excitement emerged. They committed themselves to ambitious goals. They eventually embraced 130 radical changes and implemented 70% of them during the transformation. By 2000, Lufthansa had not only recouped its DM 750 million loss, but it had also achieved a record profit of DM 2.5 billion. Many factors went into that success, but the combination of challenge and choice that the CEO handed his colleagues was extraordinarily important.

To be sure, the prospect of one's own hanging focuses the mind. But a crisis need not be a precondition for challenge and choice. Sony's Idei achieved precisely the same result with the image of a future community of Vaio users, the "digital dream kids." Convinced that they were building a creative tool for a whole generation, Sony's engineers charged ahead with amazing determination.

Note that neither Weber nor Idei used typical managerial tools to create energy and focus in their subordinates. "Motivating" people, or telling them what to do, has dismal results. In fact, such exhortations often lead to exactly the opposite of what's needed. When executives outline desired behaviors for middle managers and set goals for them, the managers aren't given the opportunity to decide for themselves. As a result, they don't fully commit to projects. They distance themselves from their work because they feel they have no control. To avoid that kind of reaction, top managers should present their people with meaningful challenges and real choices in how they might meet those challenges.

We are not suggesting that meaningful challenge and personal choice are guaranteed to turn around a failing company. Nor do we want to imply that individual managers will be able to overcome lifelong behavioral patterns simply because they're presented with challenge and choice. Nevertheless, we strongly believe it would be a mistake for a top manager to conclude about a subordinate, "John is never going to be a purposeful manager because he is just not built that way." Focus and energy are indeed personal characteristics, but organizations can do much to enhance those traits in their managers.

In fact, leaders can directly affect the type of behavior exhibited in their organizations by loosening formal procedures and purging deadening busywork. Presented with a challenge for which their contributions are essential, managers feel needed. Asked for their opinions and given choices, they feel emboldened. When corporate leaders make a sincere effort to give managers both challenge and choice, most managers can learn to direct their energy and improve their focus—and ultimately find their way to the sea.

From Disengaged to Purposeful: A Convert's Story

IN 1995, SIEMENS Nixdorf Informationssysteme was in the midst of a crisis. Facing cumulative five-year losses of DM 2.1 billion and a progressive erosion of market, the company's survival was uncertain. Internally, the vastly different corporate cultures of two merger partners (Nixdorf computers and the computer division of Siemens) had created a politically vicious, unstable environment—a perfect breeding ground for procrastination, disengagement, and distraction.

Klaus Karl, a young software engineer in the relational database part of the business, had reached the end of his rope. Exhausted by the political battles, Karl grew apathetic and began looking for a new job. He received an excellent offer from software manufacturer Sybase and was less than a month away from his planned departure when he attended a meeting organized by the newly hired CEO, Gerhard Schulmeyer.

That meeting was a call to arms: Schulmeyer reminded employees of the company's European roots, saying that it was destined to be a far better technology partner to companies on the Continent than any U.S. competitor could possibly be. Dubbing the company "the IT partner for change," Schulmeyer announced that he would give its technology-savvy young people an opportunity to take part in corporate strategic planning. Their common challenge was to help top management rethink SNI's approach to the market, to technology, and to change. Karl's name was on the list of bright young employees fingered to join the new team.

"I faced a real dilemma", says Karl. "I had an excellent offer, with higher pay and great prospects. My boss made it very clear that it was quite likely that the change effort would fail and that I might find myself looking for a job. On the other hand, if I was willing to join the change agent program, I would be sent for a special change management training program spanning three months at MIT—along with top managers, including Schulmeyer himself—and then could define my own change initiative." He weighed his options carefully, and the opportunity to make a difference proved too enticing. Karl committed to SNI.

During the training program in the United States, Karl learned to use strategy and change management tools. He formed close bonds with colleagues in the program. By the end, Karl and the other trainees—including Schulmeyer—were "committed to transforming the company."

Over the next two years, we saw Karl completely shake up the middleware development department. "We had to focus on a smaller portfolio of projects, so as to allocate our resources better," he says. "Initially, we tried to persuade people to use a new set of analytical tools. They would laugh at us. Some walked away from the meetings. Many senior people even refused to attend." But Karl stuck to his guns and continued his campaign of persuasion. "Gradually, they began to listen. They began to alter their ways of thinking about projects." As a result, a new product-portfolio analysis system was completed in a mere three months.

Karl's contribution had a powerful impact on the company's bottom line. Within three years, it successfully launched a variety of new projects that boosted the bottom line by DM 400 million. Without the contributions of Karl and other reenergized, refocused managers, SNI would never have achieved such a dramatic turnaround.

Originally published in February 2002
Reprint R0202D

What Effective General Managers Really Do

JOHN P. KOTTER

Executive Summary

A GAP HAS EXISTED BETWEEN the conventional wisdom about how managers work and the actual behavior of effective managers. Business textbooks suggest that managers operate best when they carefully control their time and work within highly structured environments, but observations of real managers indicate that those who spend their days that way may be undermining their effectiveness.

In this HBR Classic, John Kotter explains that managers who limit their interactions to orderly, focused meetings actually shut themselves off from vital information and relationships. He shows how seemingly wasteful activities like chattering in hallways and having impromptu meetings are, in fact, quite efficient.

General managers face two fundamental challenges: figuring out what to do despite an enormous amount of potentially relevant information, and getting things done through a large and diverse set of people despite having little direct control over most of them. To tackle these challenges, effective general managers develop flexible agendas and broad networks of relationships.

Their agendas enable them to react opportunistically to the flow of events around them because a common framework guides their decisions about where and when to intervene. And their networks allow them to have quick and pointed conversations that give the general managers influence well beyond their formal chain of command.

Originally published in 1982, the article's ideas about time management are all the more useful for today's hard pressed executives. Kotter has added a retrospective commentary highlighting the article's relevance to current concepts of leadership.

HERE IS A DESCRIPTION of a typical day in the life of a successful executive, in this case the president of an investment management firm.

7:35 A.M. Michael Richardson arrives at work after a short commute, unpacks his briefcase, gets some coffee, and begins a to-do list for the day.

7:40 Jerry Bradshaw arrives at his office, which is right next to Richardson's. One of Bradshaw's duties is to act as an assistant to Richardson.

7:45 Bradshaw and Richardson converse about a number of topics. Richardson shows Bradshaw some pictures he recently took at his summer home.

8:00 They talk about a schedule and priorities for the day. In the process, they touch on a dozen different subjects relating to customers and employees.

8:20 Frank Wilson, another subordinate, drops in. He asks a few questions about a personnel problem and then joins in the ongoing discussion, which is straightforward, rapid, and occasionally punctuated with humor.

8:30 Fred Holly, the chair of the firm and Richardson's boss, stops in and joins in the conversation. He asks about an appointment scheduled for 11 o'clock and brings up a few other topics as well.

8:40 Richardson leaves to get more coffee. Bradshaw, Holly, and Wilson continue their conversation.

8:42 Richardson comes back. A subordinate of a subordinate stops in and says hello. The others leave.

8:43 Bradshaw drops off a report, hands Richardson instructions that go with it, and leaves.

8:45 Joan Swanson, Richardson's secretary, arrives. They discuss her new apartment and arrangements for a meeting later in the morning.

8:49 Richardson gets a phone call from a subordinate who is returning a call from the day before. They talk primarily about the subject of the report Richardson just received.

8:55 He leaves his office and goes to a regular morning meeting that one of his subordinates runs. About 30 people attend. Richardson reads during the meeting.

9:09 The meeting ends. Richardson stops one of the people there and talks to him briefly.

9:15 He walks over to the office of one of his subordinates, who is corporate counsel. Richardson's boss, Holly, is there, too. They discuss a phone call the lawyer just received. The three talk about possible responses to the problem. As before, the exchange is quick and includes some humor.

9:30 Richardson goes back to his office for a meeting with the vice chair of another company (a potential customer and supplier). One other person, a liaison to that company and a subordinate's subordinate, also attends. The discussion is cordial and covers many topics, from the company's products to U.S. foreign relations.

9:50 The visitor and the subordinate's subordinate leave. He opens the adjoining door to Bradshaw's office and asks a question.

9:52 Swanson comes in with five items of business.

9:55 Bradshaw drops in, asks a question about a customer, and then leaves.

9:58 Wilson and one of his people arrive. He gives Richardson a memo and then the three talk about an important legal problem. Wilson doesn't like a decision that Richardson has tentatively made and urges him to reconsider. The discussion goes back and forth for 20 minutes until they agree on the next action and schedule it for 9 o'clock the next day.

10:35 They leave. Richardson looks over papers on his desk and then picks one up and calls Holly's secretary regarding the minutes of the last board meeting. He asks her to make a few corrections.

10:41 Swanson comes in with a card for a friend who is sick. Richardson writes a note to go with the card.

10:50 He gets a brief phone call, then goes back to the papers on his desk.

11:03 His boss stops in. Before Richardson and Holly can begin to talk, Richardson gets another call. After the call, he tells Swanson that someone didn't get a letter he sent and asks her to send another.

11:05 Holly brings up a couple of issues, and then Bradshaw comes in. The three start talking about Jerry Phillips, whose work has become a problem. Bradshaw leads the conversation, telling the others what he has done during the last few days regarding the problem. Richardson and Holly ask questions. After a while, Richardson begins to take notes. The exchange, as before, is rapid and straightforward. They try to define the problem, and they outline possible next steps. Richardson lets the discussion roam away from and back to the topic again and again. Finally, they agree on the next step.

NOON Richardson orders lunch for himself and Bradshaw. Bradshaw comes in and goes over a dozen items. Wilson stops by to say that he has already followed up on their earlier conversation.

12:10 A staff person stops by with some calculations Richardson had requested. He thanks her and they have a brief, amicable conversation.

12:20 Lunch arrives. Richardson and Bradshaw eat in the conference room. Over lunch, they pursue business and nonbusiness subjects, laughing often at each other's humor. They end the lunch talking about a potential major customer.

1:15 Back in Richardson's office, they continue the discussion about the customer. Bradshaw gets a pad, and they go over in detail a presentation to the customer. Bradshaw leaves.

1:40 Working at his desk, Richardson looks over a new marketing brochure.

1:50 Bradshaw comes in again; he and Richardson go over another dozen details regarding the presentation to the potential customer. Bradshaw leaves.

1:55 Jerry Thomas, another of Richardson's subordinates, comes in. He has scheduled for the afternoon some key performance appraisals, which he and Richardson will hold in Richardson's office. They talk briefly about how they will handle each appraisal.

2:00 Fred Jacobs (a subordinate of Thomas) joins them. Thomas runs the meeting. He goes over Jacobs's bonus for the year and the reason for it. Then the three of them talk about Jacobs's role in the upcoming year. They generally agree, and Jacobs leaves.

2:30 Jane Kimble comes in. The appraisal follows the same format. Richardson asks a lot of questions and praises Kimble at times. The meeting ends on a friendly note of agreement.

3:00 George Houston comes in; the appraisal format is repeated.

3:30 When Houston leaves, Richardson and Thomas talk briefly about how well they have accomplished their objectives in the meetings. Then they talk briefly about some of Thomas's other subordinates. Thomas leaves.

3:45 Richardson gets a short phone call. Swanson and Bradshaw come in with a list of requests.

3:50 Richardson receives a call from Jerry Phillips. He gets his notes from the 11 o'clock meeting about Phillips. They go back and forth on the phone talking about lost business, unhappy subordinates, who did what to whom, and what should be done now. It is a long, circular, and sometimes emotional conversation. By the end, Phillips is agreeing with Richardson on the next step and thanking him.

4:55 Bradshaw, Wilson, and Holly all step in. Each is following up on different issues that were discussed earlier in the day. Richardson briefly tells them of his conversation with Phillips. Bradshaw and Holly leave.

5:10 Richardson and Wilson have a light conversation about three or four items.

5:20 Jerry Thomas stops in. He describes a new personnel problem, and the three of them discuss it. More and more humor enters the conversation. They agree on an action to take.

5:30 Richardson begins to pack his briefcase. Five people briefly stop by, one or two at a time.

5:45 He leaves the office.

T HE BEHAVIOR RICHARDSON demonstrates throughout his day is consistent with other studies of managerial behavior, especially those of high-level managers. Nevertheless, as Henry Mintzberg has pointed out, this behavior is hard to reconcile, on the surface at least, with traditional notions of what top managers do (or should do).[1] It is hard to fit the behavior into categories like planning, organizing, controlling, directing, or staffing. The implication is that such behavior is not appropriate for top managers. But effective executives carry our their planning and organizing in just such a hit-or-miss way.

How Effective Executives Approach Their Jobs

To understand why effective GMs behave as they do, it is essential first to recognize two fundamental challenges and dilemmas found in most of their jobs:

- figuring out what to do despite uncertainty and an enormous amount of potentially relevant information;

- getting things done through a large and diverse group of people despite having little direct control over most of them.

These are severe challenges with powerful implications for the traditional management functions of planning, staffing, organizing, directing, and controlling. To tackle those challenges, effective general managers rely on agenda setting and network building. The best ones aggressively seek information (including bad news), skillfully ask questions, and seek out programs and projects that can help accomplish multiple objectives.

AGENDA SETTING

During their first six months to a year in a new job, GMs usually spend a considerable amount of time establishing their agendas; they devote less time to updating them later on. Effective executives develop agendas that are made up of loosely connected goals and plans that address their long-, medium-, and short-term responsibilities. The agendas usually address a broad range of financial, product, market, and organizational issues. They include both vague and specific items. (See the exhibit "A Typical GM's Agenda.")

Although most corporations today have formal planning processes that produce written plans, GMs' agendas always include goals, priorities, strategies, and plans that are not in those documents. This is not to say that formal plans and GMs' agendas are incompatible, but they differ in at least three important ways.

First, the formal plans tend to be written mostly in terms of detailed financial numbers. GMs' agendas tend to be less detailed in financial objectives and more detailed in strategies and plans for the business or the organization. Second, formal plans usually focus entirely on the short and moderate run (3 months to 5 years), whereas GMs' agendas tend to focus on a broader time frame, which includes the immediate future (1 to 30 days) and the longer run (5 to 20 years). Finally, the formal plans tend to be explicit, rigorous, and logical, especially regarding how various financial items fit together. GMs' agendas often contain lists of goals or plans that are not explicitly connected.

Executives begin the process of developing their agendas immediately after starting their jobs, if not before.

A Typical GM's Agenda

Key Issues	Short Term 0 to 1 year	Medium Term 1 to 5 years	Long Term 5 to 20 years
Financial	A detailed list of objectives for the quarter and the year in all financial areas.	A fairly specific set of goals for sale, income, and ROI for the next five years.	A vague notion of revenues or ROI desired in 10 to 20 years.
Product and Market	A set of general objectives and plans aimed at such things as the market share for various products and the inventory levels of various lines.	Some goals and plans for growing the business, such as "introduce three new products before 1985," and "explore acquisition possibilities in the communications industry."	Only a vague notion of what kind of business (products and markets) the GM wants to develop.
Organizational	A list of items, such as "find a replacement for Smith soon," and "get Jones to commit himself to an aggressive set of five-year objectives."	A short list of items, such as "by 1983 we will need a major reorganization," and "find a replacement for Corey by 1984."	A vague notion about the type of company the GM wants and the caliber of management that will be needed.

They use their knowledge of the businesses and organizations involved along with new information that they receive each day to quickly develop a rough agenda—typically, a loosely connected and incomplete set of objectives, along with a few specific strategies and plans. Then over time, as they gather more information, they complete and connect the agendas.

In gathering information to set their agendas, effective GMs rely more on discussions with others than on books, magazines, or reports. These people tend to be individuals with whom they have relationships, not necessarily people in "appropriate" jobs or functions (such as people in the planning function). In this way, they obtain information continually, not just at planning meetings. And they do so by using their current knowledge of the business and organization and of management in general to help them direct their questioning, not by asking broad or general questions.

Having acquired the necessary information, GMs make agenda-setting decisions both consciously (or analytically) and unconsciously (or intuitively) in a process that is largely internal. Indeed, important agenda-setting decisions are often not observable. In selecting specific activities to include on their agendas, GMs look for those that accomplish multiple goals, are consistent with all other goals and plans, and are within their power to implement. Projects and programs that seem important and logical but do not meet those criteria tend to be discarded or at least resisted.

NETWORK BUILDING

In addition to setting agendas, effective GMs allocate significant time and effort to developing a network of cooperative relationships among the people they feel are needed to satisfy their emerging agendas. This activity is generally most intense during the first months in a job. After that, GMs' attention shifts toward using their networks to implement and to help update the agendas.

Network-building activity is aimed at much more than just direct subordinates. GMs develop cooperative relationships with and among peers, outsiders, their bosses' boss, and their subordinates' subordinates. Indeed, they develop relationships with (and sometimes among) any and all of the hundreds or even thousands of people on whom they feel in some way dependent. Just as they create an agenda that is different from, although generally consistent with, formal plans, they also create a network that is different from, but generally consistent with, the formal organizational structure. (See the exhibit "A General Manager's Network.")

The nature of their relationships varies significantly, and GMs use numerous methods to develop them. They try to make others feel legitimately obliged to them by doing favors or by stressing their formal relationships. They act in ways that encourage others to identify with them. They carefully nurture their professional reputations. They even maneuver to make others feel that they are particularly dependent on them for resources, career advancement, or other support.

In addition to developing relationships with existing personnel, effective GMs also often shape their networks by moving, hiring, and firing subordinates. In a similar way, they also change suppliers or bankers, lobby to get different people into peer positions, and even restructure their boards. And they try to create an environment—in terms of norms and values—in which people are willing to work hard on the GM's agenda and cooperate for the

A General Manager's Network

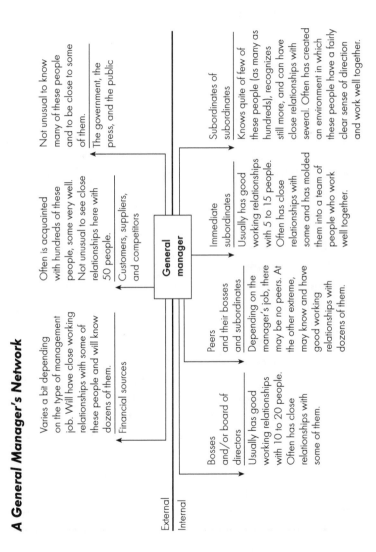

greater good. Although executives sometimes try to create such an environment among peers, bosses, or outsiders, they do so most often among their subordinates.

Execution: Getting Networks to Implement Agendas

GMs often call on virtually their entire network of relationships to help implement their agendas. I have seen GMs call on peers, corporate staff, subordinates reporting three or four levels below them, bosses reporting two or three levels above them, suppliers and customers, and even competitors to help them get something done.

In each case, the basic pattern was the same. The GM was trying to get some action on items in his agenda that he felt would not be accomplished without his intervention. And he chose the people and his approach with an eye toward achieving multiple objectives without disturbing important relationships in the network.

GMs often influence people by simply asking or suggesting that they do something, knowing that because of their relationship, he or she will comply. In some cases, depending on the issue involved and the nature of the relationship, GMs also use their knowledge and information to help persuade people to act in a way that supports their agenda. Under other circumstances, they will use resources available to them to negotiate a trade. And occasionally, they resort to intimidation and coercion.

Effective GMs also often use their networks to exert indirect influence on people. In some cases, GMs will convince one person who is in the GM's network to get a second, who is not, to take some needed action. More indirectly still, GMs will sometimes approach a number of different people, requesting them to take actions that would then shape events that influence other individuals. Perhaps the most common example of exerting indirect influence involves staging a meeting or some other event.

GMs achieve much of their more indirect influence through symbolic methods. They use meetings, language, stories about the organization, even architecture, in order to get some message across indirectly.

All effective GMs seem to get things done with these methods, but the best performers tend to mobilize more people to get more things done, and do so using a wider range of tactics to influence people. "Excellent" performers ask, encourage, cajole, praise, reward, demand, manipulate, and generally motivate others with great skill in face-to-face situations. They also rely more on indirect influence than do the "good" managers, who tend to apply a narrower range of techniques with less finesse.

How the Job Determines Behavior

Most of the visible patterns in daily behavior seem to be direct consequences of the way GMs approach their jobs, and thus consequences of the nature of the job itself and the type of people involved.

Spending most of their time with others (pattern 1) seems to be a natural consequence of the GM's overall approach to the job and the central role the network of relationships plays. Likewise, because the network tends to include all those the GM depends on, it is hardly surprising to find the GM spending time with many others besides a boss and direct subordinates (pattern 2). And because the agenda tends to include items related to all the long-, medium-, and short-run responsibilities associated with the job, it is to be expected that the breadth of topics covered in daily conversations will be very wide (pattern 3).

Other patterns are direct consequences of the agenda-setting approach employed by GMs. As we saw earlier, agenda setting involves gathering information on a continual basis from network members, usually by asking questions. That GMs ask a lot of questions (pattern 4) follows directly. With the information in hand, we saw that GMs create largely unwritten agendas. Hence, major agenda-setting decisions are often invisible: they are made in the GM's mind (pattern 5).

We also saw that network building involves the use of a wide range of interpersonal tactics. Since humor and nonwork discussions can be used as effective tools for building relationships and maintaining them under stressful conditions, we should not be surprised to find these tools used often (pattern 6). Because maintaining relationships requires GMs to deal with issues that other people feel are important (regardless of their centrality to the business), it is also not surprising to find that they spend time on issues that seem unimportant to them (pattern 7).

GMs implement their agendas by using a wide variety of direct and indirect influence methods. Giving orders is only one of many methods. Under these circumstances, one would expect to find them rarely ordering others (pattern 8) but spending a lot of time trying to influence people (pattern 9).

The Efficiency of Seemingly Inefficient Behavior

Of all the patterns visible in daily behavior, perhaps the two most difficult to appreciate are that the executives do not plan their days in much detail but instead react (pattern 10), and that conversations are short and disjointed (pattern 11). On the surface at least, such behavior seems particularly unmanagerial. Yet these patterns are possibly the most important and efficient of all.

The following is an example of the effectiveness and efficiency of "reactive" behavior. On his way to a meeting, a GM bumped into a staff member who did not report to him. Using this two-minute opportunity, he asked two questions and received the information he needed, reinforced their good relationship by sincerely complimenting the staff member on something he had recently done, and got the staff member to agree to do something that the GM needed done.

The agenda in his mind guided the executive through this encounter, prompting him to ask important questions and to request a needed action. And his relationship with this member of his network allowed him to get the cooperation he needed very quickly. Had he tried to plan this encounter in advance, he would have had to set up and attend a meeting, which would have taken at least 15 to 30 minutes—much more time than the chance encounter. And if he had not already had a good relationship with the person, the meeting may have taken even longer or been ineffective.

Similarly, agendas and networks allow GMs to engage in short and disjointed—but extremely efficient—conversations. Consider the following dialogue, taken from a day in the life of John Thompson, a division manager in a financial services corporation. It includes three of Thompson's subordinates, Phil Dodge, Jud Smith, and Laura Turner, as well as his colleague Bob Lawrence.

THOMPSON: *What about Potter?*
DODGE: *He's okay.*
SMITH: *Don't forget about Chicago.*

DODGE: *Oh yeah. [Makes a note to himself.]*

THOMPSON: *Okay. Then what about next week?*

DODGE: *We're set.*

THOMPSON: *Good. By the way, how is Ted doing?*

SMITH: *Better. He got back from the hospital on Tuesday. Phyllis says he looks good.*

THOMPSON: *That's good to hear. I hope he doesn't have a relapse.*

DODGE: *I'll see you this afternoon. [Leaves the room.]*

THOMPSON: *Okay. [To Smith.] Are we all set for now?*

SMITH: *Yeah. [He gets up and starts to leave.]*

LAWRENCE: *[Steps into the doorway from the hall and speaks to Thompson.] Have you seen the April numbers yet?*

THOMPSON: *No, have you?*

LAWRENCE: *Yes, five minutes ago. They're good except for CD, which is off by 5%.*

THOMPSON: *That's better than I expected.*

SMITH: *I bet George is happy.*

THOMPSON: *[Laughing.] If he is, he won't be after I talk to him. [Turner sticks her head through the doorway and tells him Bill Larson is on the phone.]*

THOMPSON: *I'll take it. Will you ask George to stop by later? [The others leave and he picks up the phone.] Bill, good morning, how are you? . . . Yeah. . . . Is that right? . . . No, don't worry about it. I think about a million and a half. Yeah. . . . Okay. . . . Yeah, Sally enjoyed the other night, too. Thanks again. Okay. Bye.*

LAWRENCE: *[Steps back into the office.] What do you think about the Gerald proposal?*

THOMPSON: *I don't like it. It doesn't fit with what we've promised corporate or Hines."*

LAWRENCE: *Yeah, that's what I thought, too. What is Jerry going to do about it?*

THOMPSON: I haven't talked to him yet. [He turns to the phone and dials.] Let's see if he's in.

This dialogue may seem chaotic to an outsider, but only because an outsider does not share the business or organizational knowledge these managers have and does not know Thompson's agenda. More important, beyond being not chaotic, these conversations are in fact amazingly efficient. In less than two minutes, Thompson accomplished all of the following:

- He learned that Mike Potter agreed to help with a problem loan. That problem, if not resolved successfully, could have seriously hurt Thompson's plan to increase the division's business in a certain area.

- He found out that one of his managers would call someone in Chicago in reference to that loan.

- He found out that the plans for next week about that loan were all set. They included two internal meetings and a talk with the client.

- He learned that Ted Jenkins was feeling better after an operation. Jenkins works for Thompson and is an important part of his plans for the direction of the division over the next two years.

- He found out that division income for April was on budget except in one area, which reduced pressure on him to focus on monthly income and to divert attention from an effort to build revenues in that area.

- He initiated a meeting with George Masolia to talk about the April figures. Thompson had been considering various alternatives for the CD product line, which he felt must get on budget to support his overall thrust for the division.

- He provided some information (as a favor) to Bill Larson, a peer in another part of the bank. Larson had been helpful to Thompson in the past and was in a position to be helpful in the future.

- He initiated a call to Jerry Wilkins, one of his subordinates, to find out his reaction to a proposal from another division that would affect Thompson's division. He was concerned that the proposal could interfere with the division's five-year revenue goals.

In a general sense, John Thompson and most of the other effective GMs I have known are, as Tom Peters has put it, "adept at grasping and taking advantage of each item in the random succession of time and issue fragments that crowd his day."[2] That seems to be particularly true for the best performers. Their agendas allow them to react in an opportunistic (and highly efficient) way to the flow of events around them, all the while knowing that they are doing so within some broader and more rational framework. The networks allow terse (and very efficient) conversations to happen. Together, the agenda and networks allow GMs to achieve the efficiency they need to cope with very demanding jobs in fewer than 60 hours per week through daily behavior patterns that on the surface can look unmanagerial.

What Should Top Managers Do?

What are the implications? First and foremost, putting someone in a GM job who does not already know the business or the people involved, simply because he or she is a successful "professional manager," is risky. Unless the business is easy to learn, it will be very difficult for the new general manager to learn enough, fast enough, to develop a good agenda. And unless the situation involves only a few people, it will be difficult to build a strong network fast enough to implement the agenda.

Especially for large and complex businesses, this condition suggests that "growing" one's own executives should be a high priority. Many companies today say that developing their own executives is important, but in light of the booming executive search business, one has to conclude that either they are not trying hard or their efforts simply are not succeeding.

Second, management training courses, offered both in universities and in corporations, probably overemphasize formal tools, unambiguous problems, and situations that deal simplistically with human relationships.

Some of the time-management programs currently in vogue are a good example of the problem. Based on simplistic conceptions about the nature of managerial work, these programs instruct managers to stop letting people and problems "interrupt" their daily work. They often tell potential executives that short and disjointed conversations are ineffective. They advise managers to discipline themselves not to let "irrelevant" people and topics into their schedules. Similarly, training programs that emphasize formal quantitative tools operate on the assumption that such tools are central to effective performance. All evidence suggests that while these tools are sometimes relevant, they are hardly central.

Third, people who are new in general management positions can probably be gotten up to speed more effectively than is the norm today. Initially, a new GM usually needs to spend a considerable amount of time collecting information, establishing relationships, selecting a basic direction for his or her area of responsibilities, and developing a supporting organization. During the first three to six months on the job, demands from superiors to accomplish specific tasks or to work on pet projects—anything that significantly diverts attention away from agenda setting and network building—can be counterproductive.

In a positive sense, those who oversee general managers can probably be most helpful initially if they are sensitive to where the new executive is likely to have problems and try to help him or her in those areas. Such areas are often quite predictable. For example, if people have spent their careers going up the ladder in one function and have been promoted into the general manager's job in an autonomous division (a common occurrence, especially in manufacturing organizations), they will likely have difficulties with agenda setting because they lack detailed knowledge about the other functions in the division.

On the other hand, if people have spent most of their early careers in professional, staff, or assistant jobs and are promoted into a general manager's job where they suddenly have responsibility for hundreds or thousands of people, they will probably have great difficulty at first building a network. They don't have many relationships to begin with, and they are not used to spending time developing a large network.

Finally, the formal planning systems within which many GMs must operate probably hinder effective performance. A good planning system should help a general manager create an intelligent agenda and a strong network. It should encourage the GM to think strategically, to consider both the long and the short term and, regardless of the time frame, to take into account financial, product, market, and organizational issues. Furthermore, it should be a flexible tool so that, depending on what kind of environment among subordinates is desired, he or she can use the planning system to help achieve the goals.

Unfortunately, many of the planning systems used by corporations do nothing of the sort. Instead, they impose a rigid "number crunching" requirement on GMs that often does not require much strategic or long-range thinking in agenda setting and that can make network building and maintenance needlessly difficult by creating unnecessary stress among people. Indeed, some systems seem to do nothing but generate paper, often a lot of it, and distract executives from doing those things that are really important.

Basis of the Study

BETWEEN 1976 AND 1981, I studied 15 successful general managers in nine corporations. I examined what their jobs entailed, who they were, where they had come from, how they behaved, and how these factors varied in different corporate and industry settings.

The participants all had some profit-center and multi-functional responsibility. They were located in cities across the United States. They were involved in a broad range of industries, including banking, consulting, tire and rubber manufacturing, television, mechanical equipment manufacturing, newspapers, copiers, investment management, and consumer products. The businesses they were responsible for ranged from doing only $1 million in sales to more than $1 billion. On average, the executives were 47 years old. All were male. Most were paid well over $200,000 in 1982 dollars.

Data collection involved three visits to each GM over 6 to 12 months. Each time, I interviewed them for at least 5 hours, and I observed their daily routines for about 35 hours. I also interviewed their key coworkers. The GMs filled out questionnaires and gave me documents such as business plans, appointment diaries, and annual reports.

I measured the performance of the GMs by combining hard and soft indices. The former included measures of revenue and profit growth, both in an absolute sense and compared with plans. The latter included opinions of people who worked with the GMs (including bosses, subordinates, and peers) as well as, when possible, industry analysts. Using this method, I judged most of the GMs to be doing a "very good" job. A few were rated "excellent" and a few "good/fair."

Typical Behavoir of Successful GMs

IN MANY WAYS, Richardson's day is typical for a general manager. The daily behavior of the successful GMs I have studied generally conforms to the following patterns:

1. **They spend most of their time with others.** The average general manager spends only 25% of his working time alone, and that time is spent largely at home, on airplanes, or while commuting. Few spend less than 70% of their time with others, and some spend up to 90% of their work time this way.

2. **They spend time with many people in addition to their direct subordinates and their bosses.** They regularly see people who may appear to be unimportant outsiders.

3. **The breadth of topics in their discussions is extremely wide.** GMs do not limit their focus to planning, business strategy, staffing, and other top-management concerns. They discuss virtually anything and everything even remotely associated with their businesses.

4. **GMs ask a lot of questions.** In a half-hour conversation, some will ask literally hundreds of them.

5. **During conversations, GMs rarely seem to make "big" decisions.**

6. **Their discussions usually contain a fair amount of joking and often concern topics that are not related to work.** The humor is often about others in the organization or industry. Nonwork discussions are usually about people's families and hobbies.

7. **In more than a few of these encounters, the issue discussed is relatively unimportant to the business or organization.** GMs regularly engage in activities that even they regard as a waste of time.

8. **In these encounters, the executives rarely give orders in a traditional sense.**

9. **Nevertheless, GMs often attempt to influence others.** Instead of telling people what to do, however, they ask, request, cajole, persuade, and even intimidate.

10. **GMs often react to others' initiatives; much of the typical GM's day is unplanned.** Even GMs who have a heavy schedule of planned meetings end up spending a lot of time on topics that are not on the official agenda.

11. **GMs spend most of their time with others in short, disjointed conversations.** Discussions of a single question or issue rarely last more than ten minutes. It is not at all unusual for a general manager to cover ten unrelated topics in a five-minute conversation.

12. **They work long hours.** The average GM I have studied works just under 60 hours per week. Although GMs can do some of their work at home, while commuting to work, or while traveling, they spend most of their time at their places of work.

Why "Wasting" Time Is More Important Than Ever

THIS ARTICLE GREW OUT OF a perplexing inconsistency I observed between the textbook definition of management and how real managers acted on the job. Back in the 1970s, many business school textbooks claimed that managers operated within a highly structured environment, planning their days carefully, for instance, and sharing information in a linear fashion according to a command-and-control hierarchy. But my research strongly suggested that real managers—especially successful ones—actually operated quite differently. They rarely planned their days, often punctuating them with short, unorchestrated, and even personal chats with people outside of their formal chain of command. "What Effective General Managers Really Do" sought to describe that behavior and explain why it worked so well.

Rereading this article nearly 20 years later, I'm struck that it never mentions the word "leadership." Nevertheless, a good deal of what the people described in the article were doing, especially the most effective ones, was exactly that. The language I used in this article reflects the era. We didn't differentiate management from leadership, an important distinction now. Leaders look beyond the manager's operating plans. Leaders look both outside and inside; managers do mostly the latter. Leaders communicate obsessively. All of this can be seen in the article, yet the word leadership is missing.

The article's ideas about time management continue to make sense in 1999, perhaps even more so than they did in 1982. Back then, the typical general manager worked fewer than 60 hours a week. Today executives often put in many more hours as they try to build their companies' competitiveness. Time-management experts still tell managers to compose lists of priorities and to limit the number of people they see. However, the successful ones I watched rarely did so. They "wasted" time walking down corridors, engaging in seemingly random chats with seemingly random people, all the while promoting their agendas and building their networks with far less effort than if they'd scheduled meetings along a formal chain of command. These behaviors were once valuable simply for getting work done well. But in today's intense business environment, they may be essential to prevent executive burnout and promote long-term competitive advantage.

Notes

1. Henry Mintzberg, "The Manager's Job: Folklore and Fact," HBR July–August 1975, p. 49; reissued March–April 1990.

2. Thomas J. Peters, "Leadership: Sad Facts and Silver Linings," HBR November–December 1979, p. 164.

Originally published in March–April 1999
Reprint 99208

The Making of a Corporate Athlete

JIM LOEHR AND TONY SCHWARTZ

Executive Summary

MANAGEMENT THEORISTS HAVE long sought to identify precisely what makes some people flourish under pressure and others fold. But they have come up with only partial answers: rich material rewards, the right culture, management by objectives. The problem with most approaches is that they deal with people only from the neck up, connecting high performance primarily with cognitive capacity. Authors Loehr and Schwartz argue that a successful approach to sustained high performance must consider the person as a whole. Executives are, in effect, "corporate athletes." If they are to perform at high levels over the long haul, they must train in the systematic, multilevel way that athletes do.

Rooted in two decades of work with world-class athletes, the integrated theory of performance management addresses the body, the emotions, the mind, and the spirit through a model the authors call the performance pyramid. At its foundation is physical well-being. Above that rest emotional health, then mental acuity, and, finally, a spiritual purpose. Each level profoundly influences the others, and all must be addressed together to avoid compromising performance. Rigorous exercise, for instance, can produce a sense of emotional well-being, clearing the way for peak mental performance. Rituals that promote oscillation—the rhythmic expenditure and recovery of energy—link the levels of the pyramid and lead to the ideal performance state.

The authors offer case studies of executives who have used the model to increase professional performance and improve the quality of their lives. In a corporate environment that is changing at warp speed, performing consistently at high levels is more necessary than ever. Companies can't afford to address employees' cognitive capacities while ignoring their physical, emotional, and spiritual well-being.

Iᴜ ᴛʜᴇʀᴇ ɪs ᴏɴᴇ ǫᴜᴀʟɪᴛʏ ᴛʜᴀᴛ executives seek for themselves and their employees, it is sustained high performance in the face of ever-increasing pressure and rapid change. But the source of such performance is as elusive as the fountain of youth. Management theorists have long sought to identify precisely what makes some people flourish under pressure and others fold. We maintain that they have come up with only partial answers: rich material rewards, the right culture, management by objectives.

The problem with most approaches, we believe, is that they deal with people only from the neck up, connecting high performance primarily with cognitive capacity. In recent years there has been a growing focus on the relationship between emotional intelligence and high performance. A few theorists have addressed the spiritual dimension—how deeper values and a sense of purpose influence performance. Almost no one has paid any attention to the role played by physical capacities. A successful approach to sustained high performance, we have found, must pull together all of these elements and consider the person as a whole. Thus, our integrated theory of performance management addresses the body, the emotions, the mind, and the spirit. We call this hierarchy the *performance pyramid.* Each of its levels profoundly influences the others, and failure to address any one of them compromises performance.

If executives are to perform at high levels over the long hail, they have to train in the same systematic, multilevel way that world-class athletes do.

Our approach has its roots in the two decades that Jim Loehr and his colleagues at LGE spent working with world-class athletes. Several years ago, the two of us began to develop a more comprehensive version of these techniques for executives facing unprecedented demands in the workplace. In effect, we realized, these executives are "corporate athletes." If they were to perform at high levels over the long haul, we posited, they would have to train in the same systematic, multilevel way that world-class athletes do. We have now tested our model on thousands of executives. Their dramatically improved work performance and their enhanced health and happiness confirm our initial hypothesis. In the pages that follow, we describe our approach in detail.

Ideal Performance State

In training athletes, we have never focused on their primary skills—how to hit a serve, swing a golf club, or shoot a basketball. Likewise, in business we don't address primary competencies such as public speaking, negotiating, or analyzing a balance sheet. Our efforts aim instead to help executives build their capacity for what might be called supportive or secondary competencies, among them endurance, strength, flexibility, self-control, and focus. Increasing capacity at all levels allows athletes and executives alike to bring their talents and skills to full ignition and to sustain high performance over time—a condition we call the *Ideal Performance State* (IPS). Obviously, executives can perform successfully even if they smoke, drink and weigh too much, or lack emotional skills or a higher purpose for working. But they cannot perform to their full potential or without a cost over time—to themselves, to their families, and to the corporations for which they work. Put simply, the best long-term performers tap into positive energy at all levels of the performance pyramid. (See "The High-Performance Pyramid.")

Extensive research in sports science has confirmed that the capacity to mobilize energy on demand is the foundation of IPS. Our own work has demonstrated that effective energy management has two key components. The first is the rhythmic movement between energy expenditure (stress) and energy renewal (recovery), which we term "oscillation." In the living laboratory of sports, we learned that the real enemy of high performance is not stress, which, paradoxical as it may seem, is actually the stimulus for growth. Rather, the problem is the absence of disciplined, intermittent recovery.

Chronic stress without recovery depletes energy reserves, leads to burnout and breakdown, and ultimately undermines performance. Rituals that promote oscillation—rhythmic stress and recovery—are the second compo-

---

The High-Performance Pyramid

Peak performance in business has often been presented as a matter of sheer brainpower, but we view performance as a pyramid. Physical well-being is its foundation. Above that rests emotional health, then mental acuity, and at the top, a sense of purpose. The Ideal Performance State— peak performance under pressure—is achieved when all levels are working together.

Rituals that promote oscillation—the rhythmic expenditure and recovery of energy—link the levels of the pyramid. For instance, vigorous exercise can produce a sense of emotional well-being, clearing the way for peak mental performance.

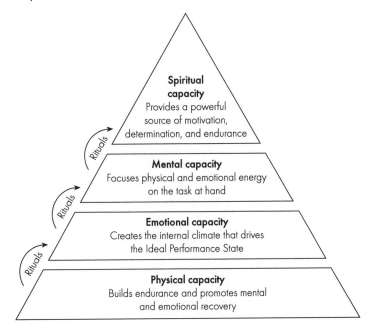

nent of high performance. Repeated regularly, these highly precise, consciously developed routines become automatic over time.

The same methods that enable world-class athletes to reach IPS under pressure, we theorized, would be at least equally effective for business leaders—and perhaps even more important in their lives. The demands on executives to sustain high performance day in and day out, year in and year out, dwarf the challenges faced by any athlete we have ever trained. The average professional athlete, for example, spends most of his time practicing and only a small percentage—several hours a day, at most—actually competing. The typical executive, by contrast, devotes almost no time to training and must perform on demand ten, 12, 14 hours a day or more. Athletes enjoy several months of off-season, while most executives are fortunate to get three or four weeks of vacation a year. The career of the average professional athlete spans seven years; the average executive can expect to work 40 to 50 years.

Of course, even corporate athletes who train at all levels will have bad days and run into challenges they can't overcome. Life is tough, and for many time-starved executives, it is only getting tougher. But that is precisely our point. While it isn't always in our power to change our external conditions, we can train to better manage our inner state. We aim to help corporate athletes use the full range of their capacities to thrive in the most difficult circumstances and to emerge from stressful periods stronger, healthier, and eager for the next challenge.

Physical Capacity

Energy can be defined most simply as the capacity to do work. Our training process begins at the physical level

because the body is our fundamental source of energy—
the foundation of the performance pyramid. Perhaps the
best paradigm for building capacity is weight lifting. Several decades of sports science research have established
that the key to increasing physical strength is a phenomenon known as supercompensation—essentially the
creation of balanced work-rest ratios. In weight lifting,
this involves stressing a muscle to the point where its
fibers literally start to break down. Given an adequate
period of recovery (typically at least 48 hours), the muscle will not only heal, it will grow stronger. But persist in
stressing the muscle without rest and the result will be
acute and chronic damage. Conversely, failure to stress
the muscle results in weakness and atrophy. (Just think
of an arm in a cast for several weeks.) In both cases, the
enemy is not stress, it's linearity—the failure to oscillate
between energy expenditure and recovery.

We first understood the power of rituals to prompt
recovery by observing world-class tennis players in the
crucible of match play. The best competitors, we discovered, use precise recovery rituals in the 15 or 20 seconds
between points—often without even being aware of it.
Their between-point routines include concentrating on
the strings of their rackets to avoid distraction, assuming
a confident posture, and visualizing how they want the
next point to play out. These routines have startling
physiological effects. When we hooked players up to
heart rate monitors during their matches, the competitors with the most consistent rituals showed dramatic
oscillation, their heart rates rising rapidly during play
and then dropping as much as 15% to 20% between
points.

The mental and emotional effects of precise between-
point routines are equally significant. They allow players
to avoid negative feelings, focus their minds, and prepare

for the next point. By contrast, players who lack between-point rituals, or who practice them inconsistently, become linear—they expend too much energy without recovery. Regardless of their talent or level of fitness, they become more vulnerable to frustration, anxiety, and loss of concentration and far more likely to choke under pressure.

The same lesson applies to the corporate athletes we train. The problem, we explain, is not so much that their lives are increasingly stressful as that they are so relentlessly linear. Typically, they push themselves too hard mentally and emotionally and too little physically. Both forms of linearity undermine performance.

When we began working with Marilyn Clark, a managing director of Salomon Smith Barney, she had almost no oscillation in her life. Clark, who is in her late 30s, runs the firm's Cleveland office. She is also the mother of three young children, and her husband is a high-powered executive in his own right. To all appearances, Clark lives an enviable life, and she was loath to complain about it. Yet her hectic lifestyle was exacting a cost, which became clear after some probing. In the mornings, temporarily fueled by coffee and a muffin, she was alert and energetic. By the afternoon, though, her energy sagged, and she got through the rest of the day on sheer willpower. At lunchtime, when she could have taken a few quiet moments to recover, she found that she couldn't say no to employees who lined up at her office seeking counsel and support. Between the demands of her job, her colleagues, and her family, she had almost no time for herself. Her frustration quietly grew.

We began our work with Clark by taking stock of her physical capacity. While she had been a passionate athlete as a teenager and an All-American lacrosse player in college, her fitness regimen for the past several years had been limited to occasional sit-ups before bedtime. As she learned more about the relationship between energy and high performance, Clark agreed that her first priority was to get back in shape. She wanted to feel better physically, and she knew from past experience that her mood would improve if she built regular workouts into her schedule.

Because old habits die hard, we helped Clark establish positive rituals to replace them. Part of the work was creating a supportive environment. The colleagues with whom Clark trained became a source of cheerleading—and even nagging—as she established a routine that would have previously seemed unthinkable. Clark committed to work out in a nearby gym three days a week, precisely at 1 P.M. She also enlisted her husband to watch the kids so that she could get in a workout on Saturdays and Sundays.

Regular workouts have helped Clark create clear work-life boundaries and restored her sense of herself as an athlete. Now, rather than tumbling into an energy trough in the afternoons and reaching for a candy bar, Clark returns to the office from her workouts feeling reenergized and better able to focus. Physical stress has become a source not just of greater endurance but also of emotional and mental recovery; Clark finds that she can work fewer hours and get more done. And finally, because she no longer feels chronically overburdened, she believes that she has become a better boss. "My body feels reawakened," she says. "I'm much more relaxed, and the resentment I was feeling about all the demands on me is gone."

Clark has inspired other members of her firm to take out health club memberships. She and several colleagues are subsidizing employees who can't easily afford the cost. "We're not just talking to each other about business accolades and who is covering which account," she says. "Now it's also about whether we got our workouts in and how well we're recovering. We're sharing something healthy, and that has brought people together."

The corporate athlete doesn't build a strong physical foundation by exercise alone, of course. Good sleeping and eating rituals are integral to effective energy management. When we first met Rudy Borneo, the vice chairman of Macy's West, he complained of erratic energy levels, wide mood swings, and difficulty concentrating. He was also overweight. Like many executives—and most Americans—his eating habits were poor. He typically began his long, travel-crammed days by skipping breakfast—the equivalent of rolling to the start line of the Indianapolis 500 with a near-empty fuel tank. Lunch was catch-as-catch-can, and Borneo used sugary snacks to fight off his inevitable afternoon hunger pangs. These foods spiked his blood glucose levels, giving him a quick jolt of energy, but one that faded quickly. Dinner was often a rich, multicourse meal eaten late in the evening. Digesting that much food disturbed Borneo's sleep and left him feeling sluggish and out of sorts in the mornings.

Sound familiar?

As we did with Clark, we helped Borneo replace his bad habits with positive rituals, beginning with the way he ate. We explained that by eating lightly but often, he could sustain a steady level of energy. (For a fuller account of the foundational exercise, eating, and sleep routines, see "A Firm Foundation" at the end of this article.) Borneo now eats breakfast every day—typically a high-protein drink rather than coffee and a bagel. We also showed him research by chronobiologists suggesting that the body and mind need recovery every 90 to 120 minutes. Using that cycle as the basis for his eating schedule, he installed a refrigerator by his desk and began eating five or six small but nutritious meals a day and sipping water frequently. He also shifted the emphasis in his workouts to interval training, which increased his endurance and speed of recovery.

In addition to prompting weight loss and making him feel better, Borneo's nutritional and fitness rituals have had a dramatic effect on other aspects of his life. "I now exercise for my mind as much as for my body," he says. "At the age of 59, I have more energy than ever, and I can sustain it for a longer period of time. For me, the rituals are the holy grail. Using them to create balance has had an impact on every aspect of my life: staying more positive, handling difficult human resource issues, dealing with change, treating people better. I really do believe that when you learn to take care of yourself, you free up energy and enthusiasm to care more for others."

Emotional Capacity

The next building block of IPS is emotional capacity— the internal climate that supports peak performance. During our early research, we asked hundreds of athletes to describe how they felt when they were performing at their best. Invariably, they used words such as "calm," "challenged," "engaged," "focused," "optimistic," and "confident." As sprinter Marion Jones put it shortly after winning one of her gold medals at the Olympic Games in Sydney: "I'm out here having a ball. This is not a stressful time in my life. This is a very happy time." When we later asked the same question of law enforcement officers, military personnel, surgeons, and corporate executives, they used remarkably similar language to describe their Ideal Performance State.

Just as positive emotions ignite the energy that drives high performance, negative emotions—frustration, impatience, anger, fear, resentment, and sadness—drain energy. Over time, these feelings can be literally toxic, elevating heart rate and blood pressure, increasing muscle tension, constricting vision, and ultimately crippling performance. Anxious, fear ridden athletes are far more likely to choke in competition, for example, while anger and frustration sabotage their capacity for calm focus.

The impact of negative emotions on business performance is subtler but no less devastating. Alan, an executive at an investment company, travels frequently, overseeing a half-dozen offices around the country. His colleagues and subordinates, we learned, considered him to be a perfectionist and an often critical boss whose frustration and impatience sometimes boiled over into angry tirades. Our work focused on helping Alan find ways to manage his emotions more effectively. His anger, we explained, was a reactive emotion, a fight-or-flight response to situations he perceived as threatening. To manage more effectively, he needed to transform his inner experience of threat under stress into one of challenge.

A regular workout regimen built Alan's endurance and gave him a way to burn off tension. But because his fierce travel schedule often got in the way of his workouts, we also helped him develop a precise five-step ritual to contain his negative emotions whenever they threatened to erupt. His initial challenge was to become more aware of signals from his body that he was on edge—physical tension, a racing heart, tightness in his chest. When he felt those sensations arise, his first step was to close his eyes and take several deep breaths. Next, he consciously relaxed the muscles in his face. Then, he made an effort to soften his voice and speak more slowly. After that, he tried to put himself in the shoes of the person who was the target of his anger—to imagine what he or she must be feeling. Finally, he focused on framing his response in positive language.

Instituting this ritual felt awkward to Alan at first, not unlike trying to learn a new golf swing. More than once he reverted to his old behavior. But within several weeks, the five-step drill had become automatic—a highly reliable way to short-circuit his reactivity. Numerous employees reported that he had become more reasonable, more approachable, and less scary. Alan himself says that he has become a far more effective manager.

Through our work with athletes, we have learned a number of other rituals that help to offset feelings of stress and restore positive energy. It's no coincidence, for example, that many athletes wear headphones as they prepare for competition. Music has powerful physiological and emotional effects. It can prompt a shift in mental activity from the rational left hemisphere of the brain to the more intuitive right hemisphere. It also provides a relief from obsessive thinking and worrying. Finally, music can be a means of directly regulating energy—raising it when the time comes to perform and lowering it when it is more appropriate to decompress.

Body language also influences emotions. In one well-known experiment, actors were asked to portray anger and then were subjected to numerous physiological tests, including heart rate, blood pressure, core temperature, galvanic skin response, and hormone levels. Next, the actors were exposed to a situation that made them genuinely angry, and the same measurements were taken. There were virtually no differences in the two profiles. Effective acting produces precisely the same physiology that real emotions do. All great athletes understand this instinctively. If they carry themselves confidently, they will eventually start to feel confident, even in highly stressful situations. That's why we train our corporate clients to "act as if"—consciously creating the look on the outside that they want to feel on the inside. "You are what you repeatedly do," said Aristotle. "Excellence is not a singular act but a habit."

Close relationships are perhaps the most powerful means for prompting positive emotions and effective recovery. Anyone who has enjoyed a happy family reunion or an evening with good friends knows the profound sense of safety and security that these relationships can induce. Such feelings are closely associated with the Ideal Performance State. Unfortunately, many of the corporate athletes we train believe that in order to perform up to expectations at work, they have no choice but to stint on their time with loved ones. We try to reframe the issue. By devoting more time to their most important relationships and setting clearer boundaries between work and home, we tell our clients, they will not only derive more satisfaction but will also get the recovery that they need to perform better at work.

Mental Capacity

The third level of the performance pyramid—the cognitive—is where most traditional performance-enhancement training is aimed. The usual approaches tend to focus on improving competencies by using techniques such as process reengineering and knowledge management or by learning to use more sophisticated technology. Our training aims to enhance our clients' cognitive capacities—most notably their focus, time management, and positive- and critical-thinking skills.

Focus simply means energy concentrated in the service of a particular goal. Anything that interferes with focus dissipates energy. Meditation, typically viewed as a spiritual practice, can serve as a highly practical means of training attention and promoting recovery. At this level, no guidance from a guru is required. A perfectly adequate meditation technique involves sitting quietly and breathing deeply, counting each exhalation, and starting over when you reach ten. Alternatively, you can choose a word to repeat each time you take a breath.

Practiced regularly, meditation quiets the mind, the emotions, and the body, promoting energy recovery. Numerous studies have shown, for example, that experienced meditators need considerably fewer hours of sleep than nonmeditators. Meditation and other noncognitive disciplines can also slow brain wave activity and stimulate a shift in mental activity from the left hemisphere of the brain to the right. Have you ever suddenly found the solution to a vexing problem while doing something "mindless" such as jogging, working in the garden, or singing in the shower? That's the left-brain, right-brain shift at work—the fruit of mental oscillation.

Much of our training at this level focuses on helping corporate athletes to consciously manage their time and energy. By alternating periods of stress with renewal, they learn to align their work with the body's need for breaks every 90 to 120 minutes. This can be challenging for compulsive corporate achievers. Jeffrey Sklar, 39, managing director for institutional sales at the New York investment firm Gruntal & Company, had long been accustomed to topping his competitors by brute force—pushing harder and more relentlessly than anyone else. With our help, he built a set of rituals that ensured regular recovery and also enabled him to perform at a higher level while spending fewer hours at work.

Once in the morning and again in the afternoon, Sklar retreats from the frenetic trading floor to a quiet office, where he spends 15 minutes doing deep-breathing exercises. At lunch, he leaves the office—something he once would have found unthinkable—and walks outdoors for at least 15 minutes. He also works out five or six times a week after work. At home, he and his wife, Sherry, a busy executive herself, made a pact never to talk business after 8 P.M. They also swore off work on the weekends, and they have stuck to their vow for nearly two years. During each of those years, Sklar's earnings have increased by more than 65%.

For Jim Connor, the president and CEO of FootJoy, reprioritizing his time became a way not just to manage his energy better but to create more balance in his life and to revive his sense of passion. Connor had come to us saying that he felt stuck in a deep rut. "My feelings were muted so I could deal with the emotional pain of life," he explains. "I had smoothed out all the vicissitudes in my life to such an extent that oscillation was prohibited. I was not feeling life but repetitively performing it."

Connor had imposed on himself the stricture that he be the first person to arrive at the office each day and the last to leave. In reality, he acknowledged, no one would object if he arrived a little later or left a little earlier a couple of days a week. He realized it also made sense for him to spend one or two days a week working at a satellite plant 45 minutes nearer to his home than his main office. Doing so could boost morale at the second plant while cutting 90 minutes from his commute.

Immediately after working with us, Connor arranged to have an office cleared out at the satellite factory. He now spends at least one full day a week there, prompting a number of people at that office to comment to him about his increased availability. He began taking a golf lesson one morning a week, which also allowed for a more relaxed drive to his main office, since he commutes there after rush hour on golf days. In addition, he instituted a monthly getaway routine with his wife. In the evenings, he often leaves his office earlier in order to spend more time with his family.

Connor has also meticulously built recovery into his workdays. "What a difference these fruit and water breaks make," he says. "I set my alarm watch for 90 minutes to prevent relapses, but I'm instinctively incorporating this routine into my life and love it. I'm far more productive as a result, and the quality of my thought process is measurably improved. I'm also doing more on the big things at work and not getting bogged down in detail. I'm pausing more to think and to take time out."

Rituals that encourage positive thinking also increase the likelihood of accessing the Ideal Performance State. Once again, our work with top athletes has taught us the power of creating specific mental rituals to sustain positive energy. Jack Nicklaus, one of the greatest pressure performers in the history of golf, seems to have an intuitive understanding of the importance of both oscillation and rituals. "I've developed a regimen that allows me to move from peaks of concentration into valleys of relaxation and back again as necessary," he wrote in *Golf Digest*. "My focus begins to sharpen as I walk onto the tee and steadily intensifies . . . until I hit [my drive]. . . . I descend into a valley as I leave the tee, either through casual conversation with a fellow competitor or by letting my mind dwell on whatever happens into it."

Visualization is another ritual that produces positive energy and has palpable performance results. For example, Earl Woods taught his son Tiger—Nicklaus's heir apparent—to form a mental image of the ball rolling into the hole before each shot. The exercise does more than produce a vague feeling of optimism and well-being. Neuroscientist Ian Robertson of Trinity College, Dublin, author of *Mind Sculpture*, has found that visualization can literally reprogram the neural circuitry of the brain, directly improving performance. It is hard to imagine a better illustration than diver Laura Wilkinson. Six months before the summer Olympics in Sydney, Wilkinson broke three toes on her right foot while training. Unable to go in the water because of her cast, she instead spent hours a day on the diving platform, visualizing each of her dives. With only a few weeks to actually practice before the Olympics, she pulled off a huge upset, winning the gold medal on the ten-meter platform.

Visualization works just as well in the office. Sherry Sklar has a ritual to prepare for any significant event in her work life. "I always take time to sit down in advance in a quiet place and think about what I really want from the meeting," she says. "Then I visualize myself achieving the outcome I'm after." In effect, Sklar is building mental muscles—increasing her strength, endurance, and flexibility. By doing so, she decreases the likelihood that she will be distracted by negative thoughts under pressure. "It has made me much more relaxed and confident when I go into presentations," she says.

Spiritual Capacity

Most executives are wary of addressing the spiritual level of the performance pyramid in business settings, and understandably so. The word "spiritual" prompts conflicting emotions and doesn't seem immediately relevant to high performance. So let's be clear: by spiritual capacity, we simply mean the energy that is unleashed by tapping into one's deepest values and defining a strong sense of purpose. This capacity, we have found, serves as sustenance in the face of adversity and as a powerful source of motivation, focus, determination, and resilience.

Consider the case of Ann, a high-level executive at a large cosmetics company. For much of her adult life, she has tried unsuccessfully to quit smoking, blaming her failures on a lack of self-discipline. Smoking took a visible toll on her health and her productivity at work—decreased endurance from shortness of breath, more sick days than her colleagues, and nicotine cravings that distracted her during long meetings.

Four years ago, when Ann became pregnant, she was able to quit immediately and didn't touch a cigarette until the day her child was born, when she began smoking again. A year later, Ann became pregnant for a second time, and again she stopped smoking, with virtually no symptoms of withdrawal. True to her pattern, she resumed smoking when her child was born. "I don't understand it," she told us plaintively.

We offered a simple explanation. As long as Ann was able to connect the impact of smoking to a deeper purpose—the health of her unborn child—quitting was easy. She was able to make what we call a "values-based adaptation." But without a strong connection to a deeper sense of purpose, she went back to smoking—an expedient adaptation that served her short-term interests. Smoking was a sensory pleasure for Ann, as well as a way to allay her anxiety and manage social stress.

Understanding cognitively that it was unhealthy, feeling guilty about it on an emotional level, and even experiencing its negative effects physically were all insufficient motivations to change her behavior. To succeed, Ann needed a more sustaining source of motivation.

Making such a connection, we have found, requires regularly stepping off the endless treadmill of deadlines and obligations to take time for reflection. The inclination for busy executives is to live in a perpetual state of triage, doing whatever seems most immediately pressing while losing sight of any bigger picture. Rituals that give people the opportunity to pause and look inside include meditation, journal writing, prayer, and service to others. Each of these activities can also serve as a source of recovery—a way to break the linearity of relentless goal-oriented activity.

Taking the time to connect to one's deepest values can be extremely rewarding. It can also be painful, as a client we'll call Richard discovered. Richard is a stockbroker who works in New York City and lives in a distant suburb, where his wife stays at home with their three young children. Between his long commute and his long hours, Richard spent little time with his family. Like so many of our clients, he typically left home before his children woke up and returned around 7:30 in the evening, feeling exhausted and in no mood to talk to anyone. He wasn't happy with his situation, but he saw no easy solution. In time, his unhappiness began to affect his work, which made him even more negative when he got home at night. It was a vicious cycle.

One evening while driving home from work, Richard found himself brooding about his life. Suddenly, he felt so overcome by emotion that he stopped his car at a park ten blocks from home to collect himself. To his astonishment, he began to weep. He felt consumed with grief about his life and filled with longing for his family. After ten minutes, all Richard wanted to do was get home and hug his wife and children. Accustomed to giving their dad a wide berth at the end of the day, his kids were understandably bewildered when he walked in that evening with tears streaming down his face and wrapped them all in hugs. When his wife arrived on the scene, her first thought was that he'd been fired.

The next day, Richard again felt oddly compelled to stop at the park near his house. Sure enough, the tears returned and so did the longing. Once again, he rushed home to his family. During the subsequent two years, Richard was able to count on one hand the number of times that he failed to stop at the same location for at least ten minutes. The rush of emotion subsided over time, but his sense that he was affirming what mattered most in his life remained as strong as ever.

Companies can't afford to address their employees' cognitive capacities while ignoring their physical, emotional, and spiritual well-being.

Richard had stumbled into a ritual that allowed him both to disengage from work and to tap into a profound source of purpose and meaning—his family. In that context, going home ceased to be a burden after a long day and became instead a source of recovery and renewal. In turn, Richard's distraction at work diminished, and he became more focused, positive, and productive—so much so that he was able to cut down on his hours. On a practical level, he created a better balance between stress and recovery. Finally, by tapping into a deeper sense of purpose, he found a powerful new source of energy for both his work and his family.

In a corporate environment that is changing at warp speed, performing consistently at high levels is more difficult and more necessary than ever. Narrow interventions simply aren't sufficient anymore. Companies can't afford to address their employees' cognitive capacities while ignoring their physical, emotional, and spiritual well-being. On the playing field or in the boardroom, high performance depends as much on how people renew and recover energy as on how they expend it, on how they manage their lives as much as on how they manage their work. When people feel strong and resilient—physically, mentally, emotionally, and spiritually—they perform better, with more passion, for longer. They win, their families win, and the corporations that employ them win.

A Firm Foundation

HERE ARE OUR BASIC STRATEGIES for renewing energy at the physical level. Some of them are so familiar they've become background noise, easy to ignore. That's why we're repeating them. If any of these strategies aren't part of your life now, their absence may help account for fatigue, irritability, lack of emotional resilience, difficulty concentrating, and even a flagging sense of purpose.

1. **Actually do all those healthy things you know you ought to do.** Eat five or six small meals a day; people who eat just one or two meals a day with long periods in between force their bodies into a conservation mode, which translates into slower metabolism. Always eat

breakfast: eating first thing in the morning sends your body the signal that it need not slow metabolism to conserve energy. Eat a balanced diet. Despite all the conflicting nutritional research, overwhelming evidence suggests that a healthy dietary ratio is 50% to 60% complex carbohydrates, 25% to 35% protein, and 20% to 25% fat. Dramatically reduce simple sugars. In addition to representing empty calories, sugar causes energy-depleting spikes in blood glucose levels. Drink four to five 12-ounce glasses of water daily, even if you don't feel thirsty. As much as half the population walks around with mild chronic dehydration. And finally, on the "you know you should" list: get physically active. We strongly recommend three to four 20- to 30-minute cardiovascular workouts a week, including at least two sessions of intervals—short bursts of intense exertion followed by brief recovery periods.

2. **Go to bed early and wake up early.** Night owls have a much more difficult time dealing with the demands of today's business world, because typically, they still have to get up with the early birds. They're often groggy and unfocused in the mornings, dependent on caffeine and sugary snacks to keep up their energy. You can establish new sleep rituals. Biological clocks are not fixed in our genes.

3. **Maintain a consistent bedtime and wake-up time.** As important of the number of hours you sleep (ideally seven to eight) is the consistency of the recovery wave you create. Regular sleep cycles help regulate your other biological clocks and increase the likelihood that the sleep you get will be deep and restful.

4. **Seek recovery every 90 to 120 minutes.** Chronobiologists have found that the body's hormone, glucose, and

blood pressure levels drop every 90 minutes or so. By failing to seek recovery and overriding the body's natural stress-rest cycles, overall capacity is compromised. As we've learned from athletes, even short, focused breaks can promote significant recovery. We suggest five sources of restoration: eat something, hydrate, move physically, change channels mentally, and change channels emotionally.

5. **Do at least two weight-training workouts a week.** No form of exercise more powerfully turns back the markers of age than weight training. It increases strength, retards osteoporosis, speeds up metabolism, enhances mobility, improves posture, and dramatically increases energy.

Originally published in January 2001
Reprint R0101H

Managers Can Avoid Wasting Time

RONALD N. ASHKENAS AND
ROBERT H. SCHAFFER

Executive Summary

THE NEWS LATELY HAS BEEN FILLED with reports
of the need to improve workers' productivity if the
United States is going to compete successfully with the
Japanese and the West Germans. Seldom, however, is
managers' productivity mentioned, although the problem
of managerial time wasting was recognized as enormous long before anyone thought of quality circles. This
problem remains unsolved, the authors of this article say,
because most cures focus on the symptoms—long meetings, unnecessary telephone calls, and tasks that could
be turned over to subordinates or secretaries. Beneath
these symptoms lies the disease: managers' anxiety that
comes with tackling innovative activities. These authors
have discovered that three requirements of executives'
jobs—organizing day-to-day activities, improving performance under pressure, and getting subordinates to be

more productive—cause so much anxiety that many managers retreat to performing more routine tasks they
already know how to do. The authors show how organizational environments permit executives to be unproductive and describe a strategy that can help them to
escape these time traps.

Y OU RECEIVE A PHONE CALL from the president of
your company. He asks whether you'd be interested in
taking on a special assignment for which you have some
unique qualifications. In this assignment you would
report directly to him, and you would participate in making some of the important strategic decisions facing the
company. The job would also involve some interesting
travel. This assignment would allow you to make a valuable contribution to the company and also provide you
with major growth opportunities.

The offer has only one catch: because the assignment
is part time, requiring about a day a week, you would
have to do your present job in the remaining four days.
Would you take the assignment?

In the past few years, we have posed this hypothetical
question to hundreds of managers, most of whom
believed that they already lacked the time to do their
jobs properly. Ninety-nine percent of them take the
assignment. By doing so, these managers are in effect
admitting that, if the motivation were powerful enough,
they could eliminate or do in much less time eight to ten
hours' worth of activities each week without negative
consequences.

Since most of these people could improve the performance of their current jobs, why don't they go ahead and

free up one day each week to focus on pressing job concerns? Because, if the managers we've observed are typical, many of them are not fully in control of the way they use time. Even though they know they should shift their use of time and attend to high-priority problems, the managers we have observed seem to be compelled to keep busy with less consequential matters. Thus, although many executives may rationally acknowledge that they do not use their time as well as they should, they cannot change how they spend it. Why? Our observation is that, to a significant extent, managers spend time performing unproductive, time-wasting activities to avoid or escape from job-related anxiety.

Every manager's job has aspects to it that trigger anxiety, i.e., psychological discomfort so compelling that the manager has to seek some measure of relief. A manager's most effective response to this anxiety is to make a direct attack on its source. For example, when feeling uneasy about an upcoming meeting, he or she could devote extra time to getting additional information about the agenda or to testing the agenda in advance with key participants.

Almost all executives, however, escape some job-induced anxiety through a variety of unproductive, often unconscious, psychological mechanisms—such as rationalization, blaming, denial, and so forth. One of the most prevalent and costly of these escape mechanisms is what we call busyness: the escape into time-consuming activities that managers find less threatening to perform (though much less productive) than the tough aspects of their jobs.[1]

Let's look at the job requirements that produce much of the anxiety and discuss their effects. Then we will examine ways managers can identify and break out of their time-wasting patterns.

Sources of Anxiety

By observing managers in almost every kind of industry, we have identified three job requirements common to almost all executive levels that often give rise to anxiety. These anxiety-provoking tasks are among the most prevalent sources of busyness we have observed:

1. Managing and modifying one's daily work patterns and routines.

2. Responding to tough pressure from above to improve performance.

3. Obtaining better results from subordinates.

PLANNING AND ORGANIZING DAY-TO-DAY ACTIVITIES

Most managerial jobs are a blend of familiar routines and innovative activities. In general, people experience more anxiety when they embark on new activities than when they engage in those parts of the job that they have already mastered .We can invoke a Gresham's Law of Time Management to describe how managers pattern their daily activities: other factors being equal, the desire to avoid anxiety will cause an executive to repeat familiar patterns and shun innovative activities.

Because the effects of this law become ingrained over many years, it is more difficult for managers than for outsiders to see these anxiety-avoidance patterns. Here are a few examples that may strike familiar chords:

- The division executive who reads and deals with all of her own mail but doesn't get around to writing the working paper on the division's strategic direction.

- The production manager who spends half of every day fighting fires on the shop floor but doesn't have time to work with his staff on production planning and scheduling systems.

- The quality control director who wades through the detailed results of every quality trial but can't find the time to organize much-needed quality improvement projects.

According to a recent survey of over 1,300 managers (including more than 500 presidents and vice presidents), such poor priority setting is common.[2] The survey reports that, despite most executives' long hours, "only 47% of their working time is taken up with managerial activities." They fill most of the remaining time with hands-on work, what the survey writers term "doing as opposed to managing." Since many of these managers worked their way up through the ranks of the "doers," their attention to nonmanagerial tasks may represent a systematic retreat to more familiar and less threatening activities. Completion of these activities becomes the measure of daily success, while more difficult and challenging tasks are squeezed out and remain unmastered.

IMPROVING PERFORMANCE
UNDER PRESSURE

Another common anxiety generator is a requirement to produce better results without extra resources. When faced with imperatives such as "reduce inventory," "increase margins," "lower costs," "improve labor relations," "speed production," or "upgrade quality," many managers are uncertain what to do. In fact, most are sure that they're already doing the best they can with what they've got and that further gains will require more (or better) people, a bigger budget, new equipment, or greater support from other functions.

Thus, when many executives hear that they must produce better results without additional resources, they tend to initiate programs without a clear strategy. For instance:

- Under pressure from their parent company to reduce inventories, the managers of a high-technology manufacturing company put their systems people to work designing a new inventory control system. Months later they found that, though well designed, the new system had no effect on inventory levels (indeed, they were even higher).

- A large manufacturing company was faced with slow growth and dwindling profits. To achieve a turnaround, top management launched a major reorganization that took two years of tremendous energy. At the end of the two years, the new organization was in place—but bottom-line results remained essentially unchanged.

As these examples show, "Action now!" often becomes the unintended pathway to more busyness.

MAKING DEMANDS OF SUBORDINATES

The third pressure that leads to busyness is the need to negotiate with subordinates for improved performance. For example, all too often bosses allow their staffs to delegate problems upward. As the boss accumulates these delegated problems, he or she too comes increasingly busy.[3]

Our observation is that this phenomenon often occurs when managers contemplate trying to get subordinates to produce better results or come up with new achievements. Some managers fear that subordinates will argue, pout, quit, or subtly refuse to produce the needed results. To avoid an uncomfortable situation, the manager unconsciously assigns the work in a way that gives the subordinate an escape: "This is an important job; I'd like you to take care of it as soon as you have a chance."

After a few weeks, during which the subordinate hasn't yet "had a chance" to do the job, the manager is likely either to do it himself or to explain to his boss why it can't be done. Similarly, in cases where the subordinate tries to do the job but the manager doubts the person's ability, managers tend to stay fully involved in the process. Ultimately, two people end up doing the work of one.

Given anxieties like these—which can arise from the real or imagined embarrassments of making demands— it is not surprising that many managers avoid framing sharp, specific, and tough performance expectations for their people. It's also understandable that they send out to subordinates signals that a good excuse will be almost as acceptable as achieving the result. But by setting expectations that have too much give or have no follow- up, no timetable, or no expectation of truly independent performance, managers become ripe for time problems. They create ways for subordinates to give problems back to the boss and keep them there.[4]

THE MALEVOLENT BUSYNESS CYCLE

The three job requirements just described are, alone or combined, sources of considerable uneasiness and anxiety for many managers. In order to minimize this anxiety, executives often escape into time-wasting activities like the ones we've described. Unfortunately, as managers succumb to carrying out unproductive activities, they neglect their principal goals and purposes. This misspent time eventually creates more frustration, pressure, and anxiety—which generates greater temptations to escape into busyness.

The culture of a work group or management team often reinforces this busyness cycle. Busyness can be contagious. It takes a number of people working together in an unconscious conspiracy to perpetuate too many time-wasting meetings, too much paper and useless information, too many people on the job, too complicated an organization structure, too many studies, and too little action. Once these activities become part of a culture, they can be self-perpetuating.

For these reasons, managers who try to stop using time unproductively will often, after a heroic struggle, find that the system has beaten them and that they cannot single-handedly change their patterns.

Breaking Away

Since evidence suggests that work-related anxiety generates most of the so-called time-management problems and that the organization's culture often reinforces these problems, no wonder the rational, traditional approaches to time management (such as time charting, time budgeting, and telephone discipline techniques) rarely have lasting impact. Short courses and prescriptive literature on time management produce temporary relief from the symptoms but do little to cure the disease. No matter how fervently busy managers commit themselves to new patterns, work-related uncertainties and anxieties still drive them to slip unwittingly into time-wasting activities. To sustain a reduction in busyness, executives need to attack not only the symptoms but also the source of the problem: the way managers plan, organize, and carry out the key anxiety-provoking requirements of their jobs.

Say a person inflicted with the busyness disease at work is on a weekend stroll by the ocean and sees someone drowning. Most likely that manager—without study groups, meetings, training programs, memoranda, or reorganizations—would toss the drowning person a life preserver. And it is not hard to figure out why.

1. The need is obvious, urgent, and compelling.

2. Accountability is clear, particularly if the person is alone at the scene.

3. The result of the intended action is predictable.

4. The feedback on the effect of the action is immediate.

These same four critical ingredients make work meaningful as well as exciting, plus they allow managers to focus on results and to use time effectively. Unfortunately, management jobs often have an absolute minimum of these zestful characteristics. Goals and objectives are often vague or confused. Accountability is ambiguous. The links between managerial actions today and measurable results later are hard to perceive. And because of ponderous organization procedures, rarely do managers receive immediate reinforcements for achievements.

Because by definition executive jobs are concerned with complex issues and with long as well as short time frames, of course managers can't become rescuers of organizational drowning victims. Nor can executives always get immediate feedback or see the results of their actions, as a lathe operator can. But managers can do a great deal to infuse zest into the way they respond to anxiety-provoking job requirements at the same time they introduce work-planning and control disciplines that minimize the chances of their escaping into busyness.

The strategy that we recommend has four elements.

1. Break a few long-term, amorphous, or complex management tasks into sequential short-term, well-defined projects.

2. Block off the busyness escape routes by gradually infusing these projects with work-planning disciplines—such as sharp definition of goals, clear-cut accountability, written work plans, timetables, explicit measurements.

3. After achieving a few modest, incremental subgoals using disciplined attacks, expand and accelerate the process. Attack more goals at once and capture a larger share of the overall job with measured work plans.

4. Then, with other managers, organize a structured effort to analyze use of time and substitute results-producing work for busyness activities. While these more traditional time-analysis steps can't solve the time-management problem, they can supplement other work-restructuring activities.

Now let's look at how managers can put this four-part strategy into action.

ONE STEP AT A TIME

Managers strike the first blow for liberty when they carve off one or two short-term tasks from an ill-defined array of long-term, anxiety-producing "things that must be accomplished" and set about to achieve their subgoals in a matter of weeks rather than months. The manager should choose a project that is focused on tangible bottom-line results (e.g., reduce scrap X%, increase output Y%, or reduce turnaround time by Q hours) and not on "process" goals (e.g., put a training program in place, get a new inventory system installed, undertake a study, or define a market direction).

For example, the rapid fluctuation of interest rates caused a dramatic increase in the number of transactions that a large bank's operations division had to carry out, and performance plummeted. In less than a year, the division was forced to write off several million dollars in overdraft interest charges. Also, despite substantial investment in new information systems as well as thousands of overtime hours, it had accumulated a backlog of 50,000 unresolved transactions. To keep on top of the situation, the senior division managers found themselves working endless hours—but the problems accumulated faster than the time in which to solve them. Eventually, the managers decided to tackle two modest first-step projects. The initial goal was to achieve, within 60 days, a four-day coverage of at least 85% of overdraft accounts. The second was to collect a specified amount of "compensation" moneys from other banks whose errors were causing the division delays in processing. Without dropping other efforts, management focused major attention on these two definable projects and achieved gratifying results. By shifting from an amorphous, encompassing view of the objectives to a narrower focus, managers could make a united, effective attack on their problems.

Similarly, an electronics manufacturer struggling on many fronts to control a costly inventory problem decided to concentrate on one category ("shipped but not accepted") and to produce a specified improvement in 60 days. And in a large teaching hospital, senior medical and nursing officers formed a small team of doctors and nurses that worked together to generate, within two weeks, more accurate methods for predicting the workload of an intensive-care unit.

In none of these cases did the managers abandon or vitiate the overall goal. Rather, as a first step, they hewed off a definable subpart that had more of the zestful ingredients we presented in our "drowning person" example. The projects' specificity, focus, and short-term nature made it easier for managers to keep energies aimed directly at results rather than scattering them in busyness.

STICKING TO A NARROW PATH

The close-at-hand nature of pilot projects makes it possible for executives directing them to introduce more work-planning and control disciplines. Managers need to define and assign each pilot goal clearly, asking those accountable for the projects to produce written work plans (even sketchy ones), concise measures, and scheduled progress reports and reviews.

Unfortunately, many senior people believe that these disciplines make good sense for the work of people at lower levels but cannot be applied to tough managerial tasks. And as long as executives define their goals in sweeping, long-range terms, there's truth to what they say. More often than not, however, by using this rationalization they avoid confronting the very essence of their work—namely, breaking down complex and abstract issues into discrete pieces. Ironically, when executives creatively and rigorously apply these disciplines to their jobs' challenges, they not only block the unproductive escape routes but also reduce the anxiety that is the source of this rationalization.

Each of the pilot projects we described was launched with a written memorandum to the people responsible for action. The memo requested each manager to come up with a written work plan that outlined steps and timetables. Methods for measuring, reporting on, and reviewing progress were also created. In the bank operations division, the senior manager even organized a one-day work session in which his department heads could reach a consensus about which goal-setting, work-planning, and review techniques they would use.

These disciplines don't need to be elaborate, just detailed enough to help managers keep themselves from wandering off the track. Without them, it is all too easy for managers to slip unknowingly into old time-wasting patterns whenever anxiety makes them uncomfortable with the task at hand. But as they commit themselves in writing to specific steps toward a measurable goal, the possibility of drift diminishes. When managers gain a sense of control over their jobs and their anxiety wanes, they become able to apply these disciplines to wider spheres of activity. Their initial successes become springboards for other gains.

BROADENING THE SCOPE

Once executives have successfully carried out a few focused projects, they can "capture" other aspects of managerial work by further breaking up big, complex, ill-defined goals and projects into achievable, short-term increments—and by organizing them with some disciplined approaches.

Thus, when one inventory category is brought under control, managers can attack additional categories in a similar way. When one production line has made some progress in reducing scrap, others can use the same processes; when one branch office has upped the number of visits per day of salespeople, other branches can apply the same approaches.

In the bank operations division, as soon as the two initial projects were clearly moving ahead on schedule, the manager of the division then asked his people to identify the crucial opportunities for improvement in their own areas. Each manager submitted an extensive list. The senior executive then asked them to concentrate on the one or two areas that would produce tangible results in the shortest time and to submit written work plans for achieving their goals.

FULL STEAM AHEAD

The final element in our strategy is to analyze and experiment with time usage directly. Managers who supplement the work disciplines just outlined with the more traditional kinds of analysis and experimentation can speed up the process.

We have found two kinds of analysis particularly helpful. The first is objective analysis of how managers actually use their time. For this analysis, managers can effectively use most traditional time management tools (such as those listed in "Traditional Time-Analysis Techniques" at the end of this article).

The second area to analyze is more personal. Here executives ask themselves questions like those in "Questions for Analyzing Time Habits and Patterns" (at the end of this article) to launch self-analysis and gain insight into the effects of certain job requirements. The extent to which a manager can discuss these issues with colleagues and superiors will influence the kind of help that he or she can receive. Managers are likely to be uncomfortable sharing this data, and it may take some time before they accept the fact that everyone exhibits some symptoms of anxiety and thus feel free to discuss these issues more openly.

With such analyses in hand, executives can shift their focus to action. They can answer questions such as these:

> What activities taking more than 30 minutes a week can you safely eliminate? Select one to eliminate next week.

> What tasks that take one hour or more a week could you do in half the time or less? Choose one to reduce next week.

> What activities that take 30 minutes or more a week could you delegate completely to a subordinate? Pick one to delegate next week.

After doing this kind of time analysis, engineers in a group working on a customized energy product discovered that they were spending 50% of their time responding to routine service problems—much more time than they should have been taking. This finding led them to shift their work patterns in several ways, such as attempting standard means of helping customers on the telephone before making time-consuming (but psychologically comfortable) field visits.

Individual and group efforts to analyze and reduce time-wasting activities lead to a kind of consciousness raising that facilitates carving off incremental project units and capturing time with appropriate management disciplines. Executives can, of course, supplement these disciplines with administrative procedures such as simplifying forms, focusing and shortening meetings, streamlining communication, and reducing organization layers.

With diligence, executives can create an ongoing process that becomes built into managerial jobs and continues to improve as it ages. But as long as human beings are managing organizations, jobs will have requirements that create anxiety and thus lead to time-wasting activities. Therefore, the strategy we've described here must be applied continually. Then the old familiar busyness cycle can reverse itself: success can breed confidence, which in turn can lead to major payoffs in management productivity.

> *Authors' note:* We wish to thank Mrs. Phyllis Connolly for her assistance on earlier drafts of this article. We also wish to acknowledge Henry Mintzberg's well-known studies of managerial time use. See, for example, "The Manager's Job: Folklore and Fact," HBR July–August 1975, p. 49.

Traditional Time-Analysis Techniques

Each manager can ask a secretary to keep track of his or her time for a week or two under a limited number of categories.

Managers can make more careful entries in their appointment books, thus using them not only as reminders but also as logs.

Executives can rate meetings according to their effective use of time.

At the end of each day, a manager may spend five or ten minutes (possibly with a secretary or assistant) reconstructing the day and noting key activities, time spent, and other important quantifiable factors.

Analysis of "deliberately planned" versus spontaneous or interrupted time is helpful.

Managers can fill out brief questionnaires about time spent in an average week or month.

Questions for Analyzing Time Habits and Patterns

My Daily Routine

Which activities of my day are the most productive?

Which the least?

How much time is spent on each?

How much of each day is simply "lost"—through frittering hours away, interruptions, and so on?

Do I have any daily routines that have not been tested lately for efficiency?

Responding to Challenges

How much of my time is spent on improvement or innovation?

How much on maintenance and fire fighting?

What should the proportions be?

Do I have clearly defined and measurable improvement goals, or are they vague?

When the pressure comes down for better results, do I ever push the "action button" or the "program button" before analyzing what's really needed?

Asking Subordinates to Meet My Expectations

What do I feel most or least confident asking my subordinates to do?

How well do I convey to my subordinates that they have to produce better results? Or do they seem to have ways of negotiating my expectations downward?

Do I get progress reports at short-interval checkpoints to make sure things are moving in the right direction?

Notes

1. For a more complete treatment of managers' escape mechanisms, see Robert H. Schaffer's "The Psychological Barriers to Management Effectiveness," *Business Horizons,* April 1971; and see Harry Levinson's HBR article, "What Killed Bob Lyons?" which appeared last in March–April 1981, p. 144.

2. Phillip Marvin, *Executive Time Management: An AMA Survey Report* (New York: AMACOM, 1980).

3. For a revealing and amusing discussion of this phenomenon, see William Oncken, Jr., and Donald L.Wass, "Management Time: Who's Got the Monkey?" HBR November–December 1974, p. 75.

4. A more complete treatment of the anxiety generated by making managerial demands can be found in Robert H. Schaffer's "Demand Better Results—and Get Them," HBR November–December 1974, p. 91.

Originally published in May–June 1982
Reprint 82303

All in a Day's Work

MODERATED BY HARRIS COLLINGWOOD
AND JULIA KIRBY

Executive Summary

EXECUTIVES ARE BUSY PEOPLE. They have too much to
do and certainly too much to read. Yet judging from the
books and magazines they buy, executives are never
too time-pressed or information-saturated to learn more
about leadership. The hunger for knowledge about leadership is not simply a reaction to the twists and turns in
the business cycle. It's a desire to beef up scarce
resources: Just as no baseball team has ever had too
many good pitchers, business has never suffered from a
glut of true leaders. Ask any follower.

In this roundtable, six experts from the corporate
world, the nonprofit sector, and academia tackle tough
questions about leadership. Can leadership be taught?
What do good leaders do, and what do they do better
than most? The discussion, which took place at the New
York Stock Exchange's headquarters in Manhattan in

August 2001, began with what leaders ought to do. The emphasis differed from one person to the next, but comments touched on three common themes: the need to formulate and communicate a vision for an organization; the need for a leader to add value to an enterprise; and an organizational imperative for a leader to motivate followers.

Conversation then turned to how leaders ought to lead, focusing on topics such as the leadership role of the generalist in organizations and the need to remain calm and decisive in a crisis. Reflecting their widely varying backgrounds, the participants drew on their experiences in the business world, the military, evolutionary anthropology, and psychotherapy to help them drive home their views on developing new leaders, rewarding extraordinary effort, and keeping organizations focused on their missions.

Listen in.

EXECUTIVES ARE BUSY PEOPLE. They have too much to do and certainly too much to read. Yet judging from the books and magazines they buy and the conferences they attend, executives are never too time-pressed or information-saturated to learn more about leadership.

The reasons aren't hard to find. If the need for vigorous, effective leadership was great when the potential of the technological revolution seemed limitless and the risk negligible, how much more urgent is that need now that the national mood has darkened and our confidence in a prosperous and secure future has been dreadfully shaken? But the hunger for knowledge about leadership predates the atrocities of September 11. Whether the times are good or bad, business has never suffered from a leadership glut. Ask any follower.

There is far more interest in leadership, however, than there is agreement on it. No topic in business is more hotly debated. Can leadership be taught? Are its skills portable? What makes a leader, anyway? More to the point, what are the most important tasks of a good leader? How do the most effective leaders invest their time? In short, what do good leaders do, and what do they do better than most? HBR senior editors Harris Collingwood and Julia Kirby sat down in August 2001 with six leaders and leadership experts from the corporate world, the nonprofit sector, and academia (see the list of participants at the end of this article) to tackle these questions. The discussion, which took place at the New York Stock Exchange's headquarters, began with a consensus on what leaders ought to do. But when the conversation turned to *how* leaders do what they do, opinions began to diverge. Listen in.

HBR: *Several weeks ago, we asked each of you to prepare a list of the three most important tasks of a leader. Let's begin our discussion by reviewing your lists and expanding on what you've written.*

Cynthia Tragge-Lakra: The first thing a leader has to do is set the vision for the organization. That's often said, but it's actually a lot harder to do than you might think. It only comes after hard thought about the capabilities of the organization and the needs of the market. The second task is to understand the changing needs of customers and employees. I've seen a lot of leaders tripped up by their inability to be flexible and adaptable, not just when the marketplace changes but also when employees change. And finally, leaders need to have people follow them. They need to energize people so that they rally behind the vision and take leadership roles themselves in bringing that vision to life.

Raymond Gilmartin: I've got a variation on Cynthia's list. I think an effective leader sees what needs to be done, gets it done, and gets it done in the right way. Seeing what needs to be done basically means that the leader has a conceptual, strategic ability to sense what's going on in the outside world as well as inside the organization. Getting it done means understanding how organizations work in terms of process as well as structure. It also means being able to choose the right people to do the job and then motivating them to do it. And getting it done in the right way means having certain personal qualities. To have a healthy organization, you need leaders who conduct themselves ethically and treat people with dignity and respect.

Abraham Zaleznik: Agreed—leaders do have to have a sense of direction, substantively, for the business. That requires taking a good long time to think about the world and understand where it's moving before your competitors do. I would say, though, that the second thing a leader needs is focus, which is what enables you to drive in a single-minded way in the direction you've decided to go. It also means being highly focused in your relations with other people, whether they're your employees or your customers or your shareholders or the people in the community where you work.

The third task of the leader is what I call identification. This is a little more complicated. I think the job of a leader is to get people to identify with him or her so that the leader becomes a presence in their minds and in their thinking. It sounds pejorative to call it narcissism, but that's what it is. Leaders need to be so aware of themselves and so comfortable with the power they possess that they're willing to let people use them as objects of identification—as totems, almost. This creates enormous cohesion in the organization.

Frances Hesselbein: Everyone so far has focused on what leaders do, and I don't think I would disagree with what's been said. But before we begin to think about what the leader does, perhaps we should think about who the leader is, because a leader defines leadership in his or her own terms. In the end, it's the quality and character of the leader that determines an organization's performance and results. Think about this in relation to the job of transmitting the organization's values. It's not enough for the leader just to say, "These are our values." If those values are really going to permeate the organization, the leader has to embody them. The army has a wonderful shorthand. They say, "Be, know, do." I believe that any discussion of leadership has to begin with how to be.

Frederick Smith: I'm glad Frances mentioned values, because that's where my list begins and ends. The primary task of leadership is to communicate the vision and the values of an organization. Second, leaders must win support for the vision and the values they articulate. And third, leaders have to reinforce the vision and the values. That's probably the most difficult task, and it's where most organizations fall apart. When people say an organization failed because of a lack of leadership, they usually mean its leaders were unable to reinforce the types of activities that lead to success and quit doing the things that don't.

Lionel Tiger: When it comes to the matter of the leader's role, I seem to have gone in a somewhat different direction than the others around the table. A leader's first task, I think, is to have a sense of the inexorability of tomorrow. Today is a wasted resource, as it were. That orientation toward tomorrow is partly a characteristic of *Homo sapiens*, who have big brains and can think of the future in a way that's very direct and very demanding. It's a difficult trick, and not everyone has the brainpower or eyesight—in a metaphorical sense—to pull it off.

Next, a leader should understand probabilities and variation. That is, you have to be able to evaluate quickly and sensibly the odds of accomplishing something. You also have to be able to look analytically at your own organization and appreciate that its activities fall within a normal curve—at one end you have dramatic events, at the other end are mundane events, and the great piece in the middle constitutes normal life.

Finally, and this sounds more obvious than it really is, you can't be a leader without followers, as Cynthia said. The fact is, all primate groups create—cannot exist without—leaders. If there isn't one, there's a period of immense tension and uncertainty, and work doesn't get done. Decisions about the wider set of environmental influences don't get made. All of the group's energy is spent on internal jockeying for dominance.

HBR: *The emphasis differs from one person to the next, but each list seems to touch in one way or another on three common themes. The first would be the necessity of formulating and communicating a vision for the organization. Then comes the need for a leader to add value to the enterprise. And the final theme is the organizational imperative to motivate followers. Let's take up each theme in turn, beginning with vision.*

Gilmartin: I arrived at Merck in 1994 after five years as CEO of Becton-Dickinson. My first order of business was to understand the competitive, regulatory, and scientific environment that Merck operated in and what unique strengths the company brought to that environment. I had a lot to learn, but I pretty quickly came up with the idea that all the information and knowledge I needed were already in the organization. So I undertook a very specific, methodical process of asking a few questions of about 35 to 40 key people in the company. What are the major issues facing us? If you were in my position, where would you focus your time?

What emerged from this process was a vision of what we wanted to do. We want to grow faster than anybody else in our industry, and we want to get there by translating cutting-edge science into breakthrough medicines. These aren't just buzzwords. Cutting-edge science means our scientists work on a disease only when there's new knowledge about its mechanism of action. With that novel understanding, they try to develop drugs that act on that mechanism. And this vision has produced results: a breakthrough drug for osteoporosis, a breakthrough drug for asthma.

Smith: Right—the reason you get results is that a vision gives you a focal point. Other things coalesce around it. For example, when everyone knows the vision, it becomes much easier to have a hard conversation with someone. Those of us here from the corporate world all work for high-performance organizations, and everyone who works at these companies knows the value we place on performance and accountability. That's part of a vision that has been communicated carefully, thoroughly, and frequently. So if an employee's performance slips, if he's not producing, it's not going to come as a surprise when you call him into your office for a tough conversation. That's one big thing a vision does for an organization. It tells people what's expected of them. And that makes it a lot easier to tell them when they're not meeting expectations. You can discuss their conduct and their performance in terms of the vision.

Hesselbein: Vision also keeps you alert. Lionel mentioned that a leader has to have a sense of the future. If we are responsible leaders, we're constantly scanning the environment for changes and for hints of how it will change in the future. This is why, for example, leaders need to pay close attention to rapidly changing demographics. Who are your customers of the future? How you answer that is going to have a major influence on the vision and the mission of your organization. It certainly had an influence on the Girl Scouts. We looked at the changing makeup of the U.S. population, and we looked at our board and our membership and our visual materials, and we asked, "When a young girl looks at our organization, can she find herself?" Making sure that she could find herself wherever she looked became part of our vision, and as a result we tripled racial-minority membership at every level in the organization, including the board, the staff, and the field.

Gilmartin: I think both Fred and Frances are talking about the way that a vision provides a framework through which you view everything that goes on in the company and in the external environment. You have to be disciplined about your activities and your dealings with other people. Everything you do is for a reason, and that reason is contained within the vision.

Merck's vision also determines the way we look at the world outside our company. For instance, we know that for the U.S. drug industry to innovate successfully over the long term, a number of enabling conditions need to be in place. One is that the United States must continue to invest in biomedical research. Another is that we have to have intellectual property protection. And another is that we need access to global markets through free trade. So we're very active in Washington and around the world, trying to shape the external environment in a way that allows us to pursue our vision.

HBR: *Along with formulating a vision, leaders need followers to help them pursue it. But to win the respect and allegiance of followers, it sounds as if leaders need to add value to the organization—and to be seen adding value. So how do you do that, especially if your skills aren't the skills the organization is known for?*

Gilmartin: Since I'm an engineer with an MBA working for a company that's strong on science, maybe I should try to answer that first. There is a big difference between scientists and engineers. When I joined Merck, it was very important for me to be able to quickly establish my credentials as someone who understood science and was aware of its central place in the company. I made a point of becoming engaged in some of the details of the scientific activity and showed real respect and interest. And that got noticed. Our head of research, Ed Scolnick, is someone who says very directly what he's thinking. The other day he said to me, "You know, when you first got here, you were more of an orchestrator, but now you're really adding value."

So apparently I'm adding something that the scientists couldn't do on their own. I'm not sitting there trying to figure out whether or not a scientist is interpreting the data correctly. I let Ed worry about that. But I am able to understand the significance of the science at another level. How does it fit into the overall vision of the company? I also watch the interaction of the scientists. What are the organizational implications of their inter-action? Who are the leaders? How does their work affect the manufacturing side of the business? This comes back to that question of focus: You have to see people and events in the context of the vision.

Zaleznik: Leaders make a mistake if they undervalue the kind of contribution you're talking about. Businesses today are in large part collections of specialists. Yet there's an important leadership role for generalists in these organizations. Generalists can take conceptual leaps across disciplines and make connections that spe-cialists can't see.

Admiral Hyman Rickover, who is known as the father of the nuclear navy, is an example of the creative contri-bution a generalist can make. He was an engineer, not a nuclear physicist. Physicists, and scientists in general, want to investigate why things happen in a particular way. But engineers see the world through a different lens—they want to make things that haven't been made before, or make them better. Rickover understood the sci-ence, but he asked different questions than the scientists. He saw nuclear power as a variable in an engineering problem. That sounds simple, but that shift in perspective had enormous consequences. Because he was able to lead people to a new way of thinking, the navy's nuclear tech-nicians shifted their efforts and energy from doing experi-ments in the lab to building prototypes. It took a whole new mind-set to build these nuclear subs, and it took an extraordinary leader to change the mind-set.

Tragge-Lakra: The term "generalist" is something of a misnomer in this context, though. In my experience,

the best generalists are specialists in some area.
Whether their specialty is marketing or finance, they
have a depth of understanding in a particular discipline
that they're able to bring to bear. Rickover knew something about nuclear physics, but he knew a lot more
about engineering.

Similarly, when you joined Merck, Ray, you had a lot
to learn about organic chemistry, but you already knew a
fair amount about managed care. My guess is you
learned enough about organic chemistry to get a handle
on what the organization was doing, but you didn't try to
interfere with the scientists. People who are new to leadership sometimes need to be reminded that they'll never
be specialists in everything and that they need to rely on
specialists to keep the organization moving forward.

Gilmartin: I don't need to know as much science as
the scientists. I can add value by staying focused—and
reminding everyone else to stay focused—on the purpose
of all our research. That, in short form, is really the job of
the leader.

Smith: Maybe I'm being simplistic, but it seems to
me that the way leaders add value is through leadership.
They're able to get people to coalesce around organizational rather than individual goals. And if they're good
leaders, they motivate people to do their jobs to the best
of their abilities and not just the bare minimum to avoid
getting fired. There are all kinds of ways to encourage
that effort and reinforce it, but the primary tool in the
commercial world is to share the rewards. Whatever system you set up to share the rewards—profit sharing,
management incentive compensation, unexpected
rewards, promotions—isn't as important as what you're
rewarding. The point is to constantly reinforce the organization's vision and values. We have something called

the Golden Falcon Award, which is a pin and a good-sized check we give to employees who go above and beyond for customers. One recipient was a courier in Buffalo, New York, by the name of Joe Kinder, who was supposed to deliver visas to a couple who were going to Russia to adopt a little boy. They needed the visas right away because the Russian government, in literally a matter of days, was going to close the window on all new adoptions by foreigners. Well, the package was misaddressed, and time was growing short, so this courier, on his own initiative, tracked down the package, corrected the address, and then went miles out of his way to hand-deliver the visas. That's the sort of effort you want to recognize and reward and reinforce.

And that's something you can track, by the way. At FedEx, we measure how motivated employees are, and we measure how well they're fulfilling the vision of delivering superior service to our customers. As for motivation, we have been surveying our employees continuously for a quarter of a century. As for the quality of our service, we have a detailed system for measuring that. We put both metrics together to produce what we call the service quality index, or SQI, which is a numerical measurement of service as seen from the customer's point of view, not from ours.

What we're really measuring is leadership. If our employees are happy and our customers are happy, those are signs that the company's leadership is communicating the vision and the values correctly and is rewarding them appropriately. That's a great competitive advantage in a service business like FedEx, where the value chain is outside the four walls. Inside a factory, you can have a six-sigma program or other quality controls to ensure that your product satisfies your customers' needs.

A measure like SQI is the equivalent in a service business. It's really your leadership quotient. If you're looking
for the value a good leader can add, that's where you'll
find it.

HBR: *Let's tilt the conversation toward the task of
energizing followers and developing new leaders.
Lionel, could you talk a little about motivation? People
talk about it sometimes as if motivation were something leaders did to followers. But isn't it more of an
interaction?*

Tiger: Absolutely. Leaders often forget that people
arrive on the scene predisposed to do a good job. I'm
always impressed with the films—they are invariably
terrible films—in which the young player rushes up and
says, "Send me in, Coach." People are hardwired to want
to be sent in. One of the things good leaders do is allow
people to do what is built into them to do anyway,
which is to contribute. As opposed to saying to the kid
who wants to be sent in, "Sure, sure, send me a memo on
that, will you?"

Gilmartin: That's right. People really do want to do a
good job. A couple of months ago, I was in one of our manufacturing plants talking to a production operator in
charge of a new high-speed packaging machine that was
absolutely crucial to getting a major new product to market on time. As I was touring the line, the production operator said to me, "I was sweating bullets until this line
got started." And I said, "You and me both."

I was so impressed by this man's level of commitment.
He recognized how important the project was to the success of the company. I give a lot of credit to the people
who lead that manufacturing operation. They have been

able to create an environment where the people on the line really believe they can make a major contribution.

Zaleznik: That desire to contribute, that desire to be sent in, really is hardwired in us. It came before there was such a thing as a paycheck or a bonus payment. And for me that raises the issue of extrinsic rewards and intrinsic rewards. I think a paycheck buys you a baseline level of performance. But one thing that makes a good leader is the ability to offer people intrinsic rewards, the tremendous lift that comes from being aware of one's own talents and wanting to maximize them.

Talent is something that we don't talk about enough. As a psychoanalyst, I often encounter people who feel as if they're floating through life. They have no sense of desire. They cannot answer the question, what am I good at? Anybody who works with adolescents or has adolescent children knows that this is one of the toughest questions there is. What a leader can do is show people by example how to answer it. If a leader has a sense of his talent and respects it, and is driven to make the most of it, this creates a contagion effect.

For instance, some people are able to look at a product and immediately sense that it isn't going to meet the needs of the people who are going to use it. And then they're able to spot the anomalies, improve the design, and create a product that people will buy. This takes imagination, acute observation, and the ability to internalize observations and use them to come up with new ideas. This is a tremendously exciting enterprise. And leaders who can pass on that excitement to their followers are tapping into the contagious power of identification, which I mentioned earlier. If you have it, people will ask themselves, "What am I good at? How can I hone my talents and make them work for me and for other people?"

Tragge-Lakra: People setting out on the leadership path need to ask themselves something similar. The first piece of advice we give to people who come to GE's management training center in Crotonville, New York, is, "Get to know your own style." We try to help each person discover how he or she is most effective as a leader. Some people are comfortable with a forceful approach, where they come in and give a lot of strong direction right from the outset. Others are more comfortable with a more participatory approach. They'd rather get a lot of input and touch a lot of bases before they start setting a course.

Whatever their styles, we can show them the kinds of meetings and review processes that play to their advantages. But we also remind people that they can't always rely on their strengths. There are going to be times when they have to step out of their comfort zones.

Smith: Getting uncomfortable comes with the leadership territory. Leaders need to be flexible and adaptable, and sometimes that means doing things differently from what you're accustomed to. You don't change everything. The principles of leadership are pretty well established. So are the principles of followership, for that matter. They're really the mirror image of leadership. When someone joins an organization, they have five questions: What do you expect from me? What's in it for me? Where do I go if I have a problem? How am I doing? And is what I'm doing important? You always have to answer those five questions, but you have to adapt your leadership style to the situation at hand. Younger people look at the world differently from people of my generation, for example, and you have to modify your style to fit this different outlook. We didn't have things like telecommuting and job sharing when I was starting out in business, but it's something that's very important to many of our younger employees. Times change and people's needs change, and we have to be flexible enough to accommodate them, as long as we don't compromise our values and our standards.

Hesselbein: You can also use your organizational structure to develop leaders. Instead of a sort of pyramid with one little guy looking down while the other people look up, you have something that looks more like a series of concentric circles. The tasks of leadership are dispersed across the organization, which releases a phenomenal amount of energy. And that's the leader's job, after all: not to provide energy but to release it from others.

Tiger: You need to be careful, though, to put your developing leaders in situations where it's clear they're there to lead, not to contend for dominance. All the energy and ambition and productivity that make some-one a good candidate for leadership development can be very destructive when he or she is pointed at the wrong target. Allow me to describe a lyrical piece of work done by one of the world's experts on chicken behavior, Glenn McBride, who's from Australia. Glenn was called in by egg producers there who were having trouble with their chickens. The egg producers had noticed that some chickens laid bigger eggs than others. They figured, logically enough, that it was stupid to have chickens that laid small eggs. Why not have only chickens that laid big eggs? So they acquired chickens that laid big eggs and put them in a chicken coop. And lo and behold, they started pecking each other to death. The producers called Dr. McBride, who pointed out that big eggs are produced by dominant chickens. Too many dominants had been put in one pen, and they were killing each other. There's a parallel, I think, to the rivalries and power struggles that erupt in the business world from time to time.

Gilmartin: There's an inevitable amount of rivalry that's going to occur when you have two people competing for one spot, and that's not all bad. But you can avoid really vicious, distracting power struggles by choosing the right leadership candidates in the first place. In selecting leaders for Merck, my goal is to have everyone in the organization agree that I picked exactly the right person for the job. And in making that selection, the will to dominate counts for a lot less than an ability and a willingness to solve problems. Leaders have to be comfortable with the idea of having a continuous stream of problems to solve. When I was less experienced, I would say, "After I get past this problem, everything out there will be happiness and peace." Then I realized that happiness and peace come from knowing that whatever problem is brought to me, I—or someone in the company—can solve it. But this is why some people don't want to assume leadership roles, because people only come to you when there is a problem. You have to enjoy the problems.

HBR: *Yes, but aren't some problems too serious and scary to enjoy? How do you handle those?*

Gilmartin: You're right—some problems aren't fun at all. But for the good of the organization, you can't let them throw you. I was in my office one day a few years ago, and someone came in with unexpected news that could have had a significant impact on the company. In the face of news like that, you have to be unflappable. You have to show that you understand completely the seriousness of the situation. But at the same time, a leader has to create an environment where people can get to work on solving the problem. It's very important to the organization that you face these situations with some sort of personal courage. If I had panicked, if I had said, "How could you have let this happen?" everyone would have frozen.

Tiger: There are some findings in primatology that have some bearing here. In chimp troops, the leader is at the center of the troop and is taking in information from all sides, from the male chimps at the edges of the troop, guarding and surveying, and from the females and their young. In fact, the attention structure of a primate group, not the distribution of resources, will tell you who is the leader. It's not who gets the most bananas—it's who gets looked at. Every 30 seconds or so, the chimps are orienting to the leader. If the leader's central nervous system isn't really calm, the other chimps get agitated and can't do their jobs.

How the leader maintains his calm is what's really interesting. Mike McGuire, who is at the UCLA Neuropsychiatric Institute, has done some work with monkeys and serotonin, the compound that produces a sense of calm and well-being and confidence. It turns out that leader primates have decisively higher levels of serotonin. McGuire's first notion was that leaders are born with elevated serotonin levels. But that turned out not to be the case. He found that when he removed the leaders from their troops, their serotonin levels crashed to well below the norm. Then, once a new leader emerged, its serotonin level started climbing until it was twice that of the other primates. An elevated level appears to be an adaptation to the stresses and uncertainties of the leadership role. And it's an adaptation that benefits the troop as well as the leader. The distinguishing characteristic of leaders is the quality of their central nervous system in a crisis. And serotonin enables the central nervous system to handle stress and ambiguity.

Gilmartin: Is that why we like the job so much?

Smith: What you call being unflappable, Ray, sounds more like courage to me. Leaders have to be capable of dealing with danger—maybe not actual physical danger but problems and issues that demand a fair bit of courage. I mean, I can be totally unflappable and be absolutely stupid. But seeing a threat coming down and staying calm, now, that's a different matter. Your organization needs to see you maintain your calm, but people also need to see that your calm is accompanied by a lot of activity. You have to be decisive, set clear directions, and keep moving. You have to show you're not immobilized by crisis.

The best leadership advice I ever got came from a sergeant when I was a young Marine lieutenant just arrived in Vietnam. He said, "If you want to know how to lead your troops, there are just three things you have to remember: Shoot. Move. Communicate." In a business context, I think that means that you have to be decisive. You have to pick a target and go for it. You can't stand still and present an easy target for your enemies. And communicate means, well, communicate. The best way to look after your people is to keep them informed, even if you have to deliver bad news. If you're looking for the essentials of leadership, there they are.

The Participants

Frances Hesselbein. Former CEO of the Girl Scouts and chairman of the Peter F. Drucker Foundation

Lionel Tiger. The Charles Darwin Professor of Anthropology at Rutgers University

Raymond Gilmartin. Chairman and CEO of Merck & Company

Frederick Smith. Chairman and CEO of FedEx

Cynthia Tragge-Lakra. Manager of executive development at General Electric

Abraham Zaleznik. The Konosuke Matsushita Professor of Leadership, Emeritus, at Harvard Business School

Originally published in December 2001
Reprint R0111D

The Very Real Dangers of Executive Coaching

STEVEN BERGLAS

Executive Summary

A PERSONAL COACH TO HELP your most promising
executives reach their potential—sounds good, doesn't it?
But, according to Steven Berglas, executive coaches can
make a bad situation worse. Because of their backgrounds and biases, they ignore psychological problems
they don't understand. Companies need to consider psy-
chotherapeutic intervention when the symptoms plaguing
an executive are stubborn or severe.

Executives with issues that require more than coaching come in many shapes and sizes. Consider Rob Bernstein, an executive vice president of sales at an automotive parts distributor. According to the CEO, Bernstein
had just the right touch with clients but caused personnel
problems inside the company. The last straw came when
Bernstein publicly humiliated a mail clerk who had interrupted a meeting to ask someone to sign for a package.

129

At that point, the CEO assigned Tom Davis to coach Bernstein. Davis, a former corporate lawyer, worked with Bernstein for four years. But Davis only exacerbated the problem by teaching Bernstein techniques for "handling" employees—methods that were condescending at best. While Bernstein appeared to be improving, he was in fact getting worse.

Bernstein's real problems went undetected, and when his boss left the company, he was picked as the successor. Soon enough, Bernstein was again in trouble, suspected of embezzlement. This time, the CEO didn't call Davis; instead, he turned to the author, a trained psychotherapist, for help. Berglas soon realized that Bernstein had a serious narcissistic personality disorder and executive coaching could not help him.

As that tale and others in the article teach us, executives to be coached should at the very least first receive a psychological evaluation. And company leaders should beware that executive coaches given free rein can end up wreaking personnel havoc.

OVER THE PAST 15 YEARS, it has become more and more popular to hire coaches for promising executives. Although some of these coaches hail from the world of psychology, a greater share are former athletes, lawyers, business academics, and consultants. No doubt these people help executives improve their performance in many areas. But I want to tell a different story. I believe that in an alarming number of situations, executive coaches who lack rigorous psychological training do more harm than good. By dint of their backgrounds and biases, they downplay or simply ignore deep-seated psychological problems they don't understand. Even more concerning, when an executive's problems stem from undetected or ignored psychological difficulties, coaching can actually make a bad situation worse. In my view, the solution most often lies in addressing unconscious conflict when the symptoms plaguing an executive are stubborn or severe.

Consider Rob Bernstein. (In the interest of confidentiality, I use pseudonyms throughout this article.) He was an executive vice president of sales at an automotive parts distributor. According to the CEO, Bernstein caused trouble inside the company but was worth his weight in gold with clients. The situation reached the breaking point when Bernstein publicly humiliated a mail clerk who had interrupted a meeting to get someone to sign for a parcel. After that incident, the CEO assigned Tom Davis to coach Bernstein. Davis, a dapper onetime corporate lawyer, worked with Bernstein for four years. But instead of exploring Bernstein's mistreatment of the support staff, Davis taught him techniques for "managing the little people"—in the most Machiavellian sense. The problem was that, while the coaching appeared to score some impressive successes, whenever Bernstein overcame one difficulty, he inevitably found another to take its place.

Roughly six months after Bernstein and Davis finished working together, Bernstein's immediate boss left the business, and he was tapped to fill the position. True to his history, Bernstein was soon embroiled in controversy. This time, rather than alienating subordinates, Bernstein was suspected of embezzlement. When confronted, he asked to work with his coach again.

Fortunately for Bernstein, the CEO suspected that something deeper was wrong, and instead of calling Davis, he turned to me for help.

After just a few weeks of working with Bernstein, I realized that he had a serious narcissistic personality disorder. His behavior was symptomatic of a sense of entitlement run amok. It is not at all uncommon to find narcissists at the top of workplace hierarchies; before their character flaws prove to be their undoing, they can be very productive. Narcissists are driven to achieve, yet because they are so grandiose, they often end up negating all the good they accomplish. Not only do narcissists devalue those they feel are beneath them, but such self-involved individuals also readily disregard rules they are contemptuous of.

No amount of executive coaching could have alleviated Bernstein's disorder. Narcissists rarely change their behavior unless they experience extraordinary psychological pain—typically a blow to their self-esteem. The paradox of Bernstein's circumstance was that working with his executive coach had only served to shield him from pain and *enhance* his sense of grandiosity, as reflected in the feeling, "I'm so important that the boss paid for a special coach to help me."

Many executive coaches, especially those who draw their inspiration from sports, sell themselves as purveyors of simple answers and quick results.

Executive coaching further eroded Bernstein's performance, as often occurs when narcissists avoid the truth.

My misgivings about executive coaching are not a clarion call for psychotherapy or psychoanalysis. Psychoanalysis, in particular, does not—and never will—suit everybody. Nor is it up to corporate leaders to ensure that all employees deal with their personal demons. My goal, as someone with a doctorate in psychology who also serves as an executive coach, is to heighten awareness of the difference between a "problem executive" who can be trained to function effectively and an "executive with a problem" who can best be helped by psychotherapy.

The issue is threefold. First, many executive coaches, especially those who draw their inspiration from sports, sell themselves as purveyors of simple answers and quick results. Second, even coaches who accept that an executive's problems may require time to address still tend to rely solely on behavioral solutions. Finally, executive coaches unschooled in the dynamics of psychotherapy often exploit the powerful hold they develop over their clients. Sadly, misguided coaching ignores—and even creates—deep-rooted psychological problems that often only psychotherapy can fix.

The Lure of Easy Answers

The popularity of executive coaching owes much to the modern craze for easy answers. Businesspeople in general—and American ones in particular—constantly look for new ways to change as quickly and painlessly as possible. Self-help manuals abound. Success is defined in 12 simple steps or seven effective habits. In this environment of quick fixes, psychotherapy has become marginalized. And executive coaches have stepped in to fill the gap, offering a kind of instant alternative. As management guru Warren Bennis observes, "A lot of executive coaching is really an acceptable form of psychotherapy. It's still tough to say, 'I'm going to see my therapist.' It's okay to say, 'I'm getting counseling from my coach.'"

To achieve fast results, many popular executive coaches model their interventions after those used by sports coaches, employing techniques that reject out of hand any introspective process that can take time and cause "paralysis by analysis." The idea that an executive coach can help employees improve performance quickly is a great selling point to CEOs, who put the bottom line first. Yet that approach tends to gloss over any unconscious conflict the employee might have. This can have disastrous consequences for the company in the long term and can exacerbate the psychological damage to the person targeted for help.

Consider Jim Mirabella, an executive earmarked for leadership at an electronic games manufacturer. Ever since the CEO had promoted him to head of marketing, Mirabella had become impossible to work with. Colleagues complained that he hoarded information about company strategy, market indicators, sales forecasts, and the like. The theory circulating through the grapevine was that Mirabella's aim was to weaken junior executives' ability to make informed contributions during interdivisional strategic-planning sessions. He was assigned an executive coach.

At first meeting, coach Sean McNulty was impressive. He had a bodybuilder's physique and a model's face. Although he had been cocaptain of the football team at the Big Ten university he had attended, McNulty always knew that he was too small for professional sports and not studious enough for medicine or law. But realizing he had charisma to spare, McNulty decided, while an undergraduate business major minoring in sports psychology, that he would pursue a career in executive coaching. After earning an MBA from a leading university, McNulty soon became known in the local business community as a man who could polish the managerial skills of even the ugliest of ducklings.

McNulty's mandate was to shadow Mirabella 24/7 for as long as needed to ensure that he would grow into his position. From the start of their relationship, McNulty and Mirabella had two private meetings a day during which McNulty analyzed Mirabella's behavior and role-played effective styles for mastering interpersonal situations that Mirabella did not handle well. True to his jock background, McNulty reacted to Mirabella's avowals of ineptitude and anxiety with exhortations. "Quitters never win, and winners never quit" was a favorite comment of his, but at times McNulty would also chide Mirabella for being a "weakling" who needed to "act like a man" to deal with the demands of his preordained role within the company.

By dint of McNulty's force of personality or indefatigability, Mirabella stopped fighting his coach's efforts to toughen him up. To all outward appearances, Mirabella began acting like the assertive executive he wasn't. Once McNulty saw Mirabella's behavior change, he told the CEO that Mirabella was now up to the job. But within a week of ending his meetings with McNulty, Mirabella became severely depressed. At that point, he turned to me for help.

I soon realized that Mirabella wasn't trying to sabotage his colleagues in order to get ahead. In fact, he felt he was moving ahead too fast. Mirabella was convinced that he had only been promoted because, like the company's CEO, he was an Italian-American. Mirabella believed that he hadn't earned his success but had it imposed on him because of the CEO's wish for an appropriate heir to the throne. As a result, Mirabella felt enormously anxious and angry. "Why should I be forced to overachieve just so I can fulfill my boss's dream to keep the company in the hands of Italians?" he demanded.

An even more important component of Mirabella's emotional struggle, though, was his morbid fear of failure. He obsessed that the leadership style he had developed belonged to his coach—not to him—and he dreaded being exposed as a fake.

Had Mirabella's coach been less sports driven—or better versed in interpersonal psychology—he could have anticipated that all the learned bravado in the world could never prepare Mirabella for the role he was assigned to fill. Mirabella needed someone who would listen to his fears and analyze their origins. In the end, Mirabella could function effectively only if his advancement was predicated on his own desires and leadership style—not on someone else's. Once he was able to deal with his inner conflicts related to those issues, Mirabella's career proceeded without incident.

The Snare of Behaviorism

Even when coaches adopt a more empirically validated approach than McNulty did, they still tend to fall into the trap of treating the symptoms rather than the disorder. That's because they typically derive their treatments from behavioral psychology. Of course, behaviorism has been a great boon to psychiatry in recent years. Findings from this discipline have helped people enormously in controlling specific behaviors and learning to cope in particular situations. But treatments derived from behavioral psychology are sometimes too limited to address the problems that disrupt executives' ability to function.

One of the most popular behaviorist solutions is assertiveness training. This technique is most often used to help individuals cope with situations that evoke intense negative feelings—for example, helping drug addicts to "just say no" to temptation. Executive coaches use assertiveness training in a number of contexts. For instance, many coaches working with executives who appear to be lacking confidence employ the technique in an effort to get them to perform better. Unfortunately, learning effective responses to stressors often fails to help corporate executives deal with their intrapsychic pressures.

Take Jennifer Mansfield, vice president of training and development at a large software manufacturer. An acknowledged workaholic, Mansfield had followed a traditional path within her corporation, rising through the ranks by fulfilling every assignment with stellar results. When she was promoted to a managerial position, however, Mansfield's self-confidence began to slip. As a boss, she found it hard to delegate. Accustomed to delivering 110%, she was loath to cede control to her direct reports. She also found it impossible to give negative feedback. As a consequence, her work and that of her subordinates started to suffer, and she was missing deadlines.

Her boss presumed Mansfield was having an assertiveness problem, so he hired a coach from a consulting firm that specialized in behavioral treatments to work with her. The coach assumed that Mansfield needed to learn to set limits, to constructively criticize her subordinates, and to avoid the trap of doing other people's work for them. Within two months of what her coach deemed successful training, Mansfield began to lose weight, grow irritable, and display signs of exhaustion. At the time, I happened to be coaching the software company's COO, and he asked me to talk to her. It didn't take long to see how assertiveness training had unearthed a problem Mansfield had managed to keep under wraps for years.

Companies have a very tough time dealing with workaholics like Mansfield. Such individuals tend to sacrifice social and avocational pursuits in favor of work, and businesses value their productivity. It's hard to realize that these people have struck a Faustian bargain: trading success for "a life." Mansfield became a workaholic because she harbored a tremendous fear of intimacy. Although she was young, attractive, and likable, her parents' divorce and her mother's subsequent emotional suffering (communicated to Mansfield as "all men are bastards") left her fearful of forming intimate relationships with men. Those were easy for her to avoid when she managed discrete projects by putting in 80-hour work-weeks. But Mansfield could no longer do so when she became the manager of 11 professionals, seven of whom were men. For the first time in her career, males were showering her with attention, and the consequences were extremely disruptive.

Many coaches gain a Svengali-like hold over both the executives they train and the CEOs they report to, sometimes with disastrous consequences.

Mansfield could neither comprehend nor cope with the attention she received once promoted to the role of boss. While most managers would view the schmoozing and lobbying for attention that her reports engaged in as office politics, Mansfield saw these attempts at currying favor as trial balloons that might lead to dating. She was not being sexually harassed; Mansfield was merely expe-

riencing interpersonal advances that threatened the
protective fortress she had erected against feelings of
intimacy. The better Mansfield managed the men in her
division—and the more her constructive feedback
improved their work—the more intimate they appeared
to become as a natural outcome of their appreciation.

I passed this diagnosis along to the executive vice
president of human resources, and he concurred. Mansfield's coaching ceased, and after her boss and I conducted a carefully crafted intervention, she agreed to
seek outpatient psychotherapy. Several years later,
Mansfield was thriving as a manager, and she had developed a more fulfilling personal life.

Not all executive coaches are as indifferent as Mansfield's was to underlying psychological disturbances. But
those oversights are common when coaches focus on
problems rather than people. Such coaches tend to
define the problems plaguing an executive in the terms
they understand best. If all you have is a hammer, everything looks like a nail.

The Trap of Influence

Executive coaches are at their most dangerous when
they win the CEO's ear. This puts them in a position to
wield great power over an entire organization, a scenario
that occurs with disturbing frequency. Since many executive coaches were corporate types in prior lives, they
connect with CEOs far more readily than most psychotherapists do. They are fluent in business patois, and
they move easily from discussions of improving an individual's performance to conducting interventions that
can help entire business units capture or retain market
share. Unless these executive coaches have been trained

in the dynamics of interpersonal relations, however, they may abuse their power—often without meaning to. Indeed, many coaches gain a Svengali-like hold over both the executives they train and the CEOs they report to, sometimes with disastrous consequences.

Take Rich Garvin, the CEO of an athletic shoe manufacturing company with sales in excess of $100 million a year. Despite his company's size, Garvin had never hired a coach for any of his direct reports. He knew that his HR director used trainers and coaches, but Garvin was a finance guy first and foremost. And since the athletic shoe industry was flying high, he left personnel matters to those who were paid to worry about them. But in the late 1990s, the market for athletic shoes collapsed. In Garvin's world, the most immediate casualty was his COO, who snapped under the strain of failing to meet sales estimates for three consecutive quarters. The COO began venting his frustration on store managers, buyers, and suppliers.

Garvin was under the gun during this difficult time, so he skipped the usual steps and sought the services of an executive coach on his own. He picked someone he knew well: Karl Nelson, whom Garvin had worked with at a major consulting firm when they were both starting their careers as freshly minted MBAs. Garvin thought he could trust Nelson to help manage his COO's anger and to mentor him through the storm. He also liked the sound of Nelson's coaching approach. It was based on a profiling system that diagnosed managers' strengths and weaknesses and charted career tracks that would optimize individual managers' productivity. This system was similar to the Myers-Briggs inventory, with many of psychologist Abraham Maslow's self-actualization principles thrown in. Garvin believed that Nelson and his system could help the COO.

Within six months of taking the assignment, Nelson claimed that the once-raging COO was calm and capable of fulfilling his duties. While this successful outcome was aided in large part by the athletic shoe industry's recovery, Garvin was nevertheless impressed with his friend's accomplishments. When Nelson suggested that he apply the profiling system to all the company's key executives, Garvin didn't give it a second thought.

During the next year, Nelson suggested a number of personnel changes. Since those came with the CEO's backing, the HR director accepted them, no questions asked. Because she was afraid to buck the CEO's hand-picked adviser, the personnel director also said nothing about the problems that ensued. These stemmed from Nelson's exclusive reliance on his profiling system. For example, in recommending the promotion of one East Coast store manager to regional director of West Coast sales, Nelson ignored the man's unfamiliarity with the region and the people he was appointed to manage. Not surprisingly, that move—and many of Nelson's other ill-conceived selections—bombed. To compound the problem, word of Nelson's status and his often horrific recommendations circulated through the company like wildfire, leading many people to both fear and resent his undue influence over Garvin. The negative emotions Nelson generated were so intense that underperforming, newly promoted managers became the targets of an undeclared, but uniformly embraced, pattern of passive-aggressive behavior by the rank and file. Such behaviors ranged from not attending meetings to botching orders to failing to stock goods in a timely manner.

Psychiatrists who've studied the Vietnam War are all too familiar with this type of hostile reaction to ineffectual leaders. Lieutenants fresh from ROTC training were hazed, sometimes even killed, by veteran troops who resented what they perceived to be an illegitimate attempt by the "F—ing New Guy" (FNG) to exercise authority. Military psychiatrists soon realized that these FNG lieutenants, clueless about the laws that governed life on the front lines, had been pulling rank in an effort to assert authority. The troopers did not take this well. In their view, the new lieutenants did not stack up to their predecessors, who had learned to let their hair down. To address the FNG syndrome, the military cautioned lieutenants to take it easy until the troopers accepted that they had developed field credentials.

When Garvin was confronted by a second decline in sales, this one precipitated by the FNG syndrome, he had no idea that Nelson's activities had caused the problem. In fact, because he believed that Nelson was expert in all matters of personnel functioning and efficiency, Garvin *increased* his reliance on his friend's counsel. He had become a victim of what, in the language of psychiatry, is called "transference"—a dynamic that gave Nelson extraordinary psychological power over Garvin.

Most people understand transference as "falling in love" with one's therapist. While this can be a manifestation, it paints an incomplete picture of the phenomenon. Transference can be positive or negative. Essentially, it is a powerful feeling for someone whose traits mirror those of a significant person—typically a parent—from one's past. Garvin formed a positive transference toward Nelson (who "saved" his COO). That placed Garvin in the role of an information-dependent child vis-à-vis an expert parent. Garvin relied on his coach to come up with best practices for handling problem executives. CEOs often form these sorts of relationships with their coaches.

Not all CEOs experience transference. Even so, coaches can easily expand their influence—from training to all-purpose advising—because CEOs don't like to lose face. Company leaders understand what coaches do and often feel personally responsible for selecting them. As a result, they feel more accountable for their coaches' successes or failures than they would if a psychotherapist were assigned to the case. In the same vein, when the CEO personally endorses a business plan, a number of psychological factors conspire to make it difficult to abandon that plan. Garvin was confronted with that situation when he authorized systemwide use of Nelson's personnel development procedures.

Garvin's story had a happy ending. Eventually he was persuaded to bring in a consulting firm to address the problems besetting his company. On the consultants' recommendation, he terminated Nelson's contract, and the FNG syndrome ceased. Not all CEOs are that lucky.

The Importance of Expertise

To best help their executives, companies need to draw on the expertise of both psychotherapists and executive coaches with legitimate skills. At a minimum, every executive slated to receive coaching should first receive a psychological evaluation. By screening out employees not psychologically prepared or predisposed to benefit from the process, companies avoid putting executives in deeply uncomfortable—even damaging—positions. Equally important, companies should hire independent mental health professionals to review coaching outcomes. This helps to ensure that coaches are not ignoring underlying problems or creating new ones, as Nelson did.

Psychological assessment and treatment are no silver bullet—and can in fact be gratuitous. For instance, a coach who trains executives to enhance their strategic-planning abilities need not be a psychiatrist. But don't assume that all executives who have planning problems lack the necessary skills. Can a psychological disorder interfere with developing a business plan? Absolutely, if the client suffers from clinical depression, which is known to block one's ability to engage in constructive, goal-oriented behavior. Without safeguards to prevent coaches from training those whose problems stem not from a lack of skills but from psychological problems, the executives being coached and the companies they work for will suffer.

The Economics of Executive Coaching

EXECUTIVE COACHING IS a major growth industry. At least 10,000 coaches work for businesses today, up from 2,000 in 1996. And that figure is expected to exceed 50,000 in the next five years. Executive coaching is also highly profitable; employers are now willing to pay fees ranging from $1,5000 to $15,000 a day. That's a lot more than any psychotherapist could even dream of charging. Why are companies willing to pay so much more for their coaches?

The answer is simple: Executive coaches offer seemingly quick and easy solutions. CEOs tell me that what they fear most about psychotherapy is not the cost in dollars but the cost in time. A coaching engagement typically lasts no more then six months. Psychotherapy, by contrast, is seen as long-term treatment; people joke that it takes six moths for a therapist and patient just to say hello. What's more, therapy requires a greater time commitment than the standard 50-minute sessions; it also involves travel to and from the therapist's office, taking even more time away from work.

If coaching fails to cure a problem in six months, it can become very expensive indeed. Take the case of Tom Davis, the coach who worked with Rob Bernstein, the executive VP of sales at an automotive parts distributor. Let's assume Davis charged a relatively low per diem of $1,500. Over the four years of his engagement—which ultimately did not solve Bernstein's problems—he would have picked up at least $45,000 in fees. That sum would have purchased 450 hours with a competent therapist—about ten years' worth of weekly sessions.

Originally published in June 2002
Reprint R0206E

Saving Your Rookie Managers from Themselves

CAROL A. WALKER

Executive Summary

MOST ORGANIZATIONS PROMOTE employees into managerial positions based on their technical competence. But very often, that kind of competence does not translate into good managerial performance. Many rookie managers fail to grasp how their roles have changed: that their jobs are no longer about personal achievement but about enabling others to achieve, that sometimes driving the bus means taking a backseat, and that building a team is often more important than cutting a deal. Even the best employees have trouble adjusting to these new realities, and that trouble can be exacerbated by the normal insecurities that may make rookie managers hesitant to ask for help.

The dynamic unfolds something like this: As rookie managers internalize their stress, their focus, too, becomes increasingly internal. They become insecure and self-focused and cannot properly support their teams. Invariably, trust breaks down, staff members become alienated, and productivity suffers.

In this article, coach and management consultant Carol Walker, who works primarily with rookie managers and their supervisors, addresses the five problem areas that rookie managers typically face: delegating, getting support from senior staffers, projecting confidence, thinking strategically, and giving feedback. You may think these elements sound like Management 101, and you'd be right, Walker writes. But these basic elements are also what trip up most managers in the early stages of their careers (and even, she admits, throughout their careers). The bosses of rookie managers have a responsibility to anticipate and address these problems; not doing so will hurt the rookie, the boss, and the company overall.

TOM EDELMAN, like a million freshly minted managers before him, had done a marvelous job as an individual contributor. He was smart, confident, forward thinking, and resourceful. His clients liked him, as did his boss and coworkers. Consequently, no one in the department was surprised when his boss offered him a managerial position. Tom accepted with some ambivalence—he loved working directly with clients and was loath to give that up—but on balance, he was thrilled.

Six months later, when I was called in to coach Tom (I've disguised his name), I had trouble even picturing the confident insider he once had been. He looked like a deer caught in the headlights. Tom seemed overwhelmed and indeed even used that word several times to describe how he felt. He had started to doubt his abilities. His direct reports, once close colleagues, no longer seemed to respect or even like him. What's more, his department had been beset by a series of small crises, and Tom spent most of his time putting out these fires. He knew this wasn't the most effective use of his time, but he didn't know how to stop. These problems hadn't yet translated into poor business results, but he was in trouble nonetheless.

His boss realized that he was in danger of failing and brought me in to assist. With support and coaching, Tom got the help he needed and eventually became an effective manager. Indeed, he has been promoted twice since I worked with him, and he now runs a small division within the same company. But his near failure—and the path that brought him to that point—is surprisingly typical. Most organizations promote employees into managerial positions based on their technical competence. Very often, however, those people fail to grasp how their roles have changed—that their jobs are no longer about personal achievement but instead about enabling others to achieve, that sometimes driving the bus means taking a backseat, and that building a team is often more important than cutting a deal. Even the best employees can have trouble adjusting to these new realities. That trouble may be exacerbated by normal insecurities that make rookie managers hesitant to ask for help, even when they find themselves in thoroughly unfamiliar territory. As these new managers internalize their stress, their focus becomes internal as well. They become insecure and self-focused and cannot properly support their teams. Inevitably, trust breaks down, staff members are alienated, and productivity suffers.

Many companies unwittingly support this downward spiral by assuming that their rookie managers will somehow learn critical management skills by osmosis. Some rookies do, to be sure, but in my experience they're the exceptions. Most need more help. In the absence of comprehensive training and intensive coaching—which most companies don't offer—the rookie manager's boss plays a key role. Of course, it's not possible for most senior managers to spend hours and hours every week overseeing a new manager's work, but if you know what typical challenges a rookie manager faces, you'll be able to anticipate some problems before they arise and nip others in the bud.

Delegating

Effective delegation may be one of the most difficult tasks for rookie managers. Senior managers bestow on them big responsibilities and tight deadlines, and they put a lot of pressure on them to produce results. The natural response of rookies when faced with such challenges is to "just do it," thinking that's what got them promoted in the first place. But their reluctance to delegate assignments also has its roots in some very real fears. First is the fear of losing stature: If I assign high-profile projects to my staff members, they'll get the credit. What kind of visibility will I be left with? Will it be clear to my boss and my staff what value I'm adding? Second is the fear of abdicating control: If I allow Frank to do this, how can I be sure that he will do it correctly? In the face of this fear, the rookie manager may delegate tasks but supervise Frank so closely that he will never feel accountable. Finally, the rookie may be hesitant to delegate work because he's afraid of overburdening his staff. He may be uncomfortable assigning work to former peers for fear that they'll resent him. But the real resentment usually comes when staff members feel that lack of opportunity is blocking their advancement.

Signs that these fears may be playing out include new managers who work excessively long hours, are hesitant to take on new responsibilities, have staff members who seem unengaged, or have a tendency to answer on behalf of employees instead of encouraging them to communicate with you directly.

The first step toward helping young managers delegate effectively is to get them to understand their new role. Acknowledge that their job fundamentally differs from an individual contributor's. Clarify what you and the organization value in leaders. Developing talented, promotable staff is critical in any company. Let new managers know that they will be rewarded for these less tangible efforts in addition to hitting numerical goals. Understanding this new role is half the battle for rookie managers, and one that many companies mistakenly assume is evident from the start.

After clarifying how your rookie manager's role has changed, you can move on to tactics. Perhaps it goes without saying, but you should lead by example. You have the responsibility to empower the rookie who works for you and do what you can to help him overcome his insecurities about his value to the organization. You can then assist him in looking for opportunities to empower and engage his team.

One young manager I worked with desperately needed to find time to train and supervise new employees. His firm had been recently acquired, and he had to deal with high staff turnover and new industrywide rules and regulations. The most senior person on his staff—a woman who had worked for the acquiring company— was about to return from an extended family leave, and he was convinced that he couldn't ask her for help. After all, she had a part-time schedule, and she'd asked to be assigned to the company's largest client. To complicate matters, he suspected that she resented his promotion. As we evaluated the situation, the manager was able to see that the senior staffer's number one priority was reestablishing herself as an important part of the team. Once he realized this, he asked her to take on critical supervisory responsibilities, balanced with a smaller client load, and she eagerly agreed. Indeed, she returned from leave excited about partnering with her manager to develop the team.

When a new manager grumbles about mounting workloads, seize the opportunity to discuss delegation. Encourage him to take small risks initially, playing to the obvious strengths of his staff members. Asking his super-organized, reliable assistant to take the lead in handling the logistics of a new product launch, for example, is much less risky than asking a star salesperson, unaccustomed to this sort of detailed work, to do it. Early successes will build the manager's confidence and willingness to take progressively larger risks in stretching each team member's capabilities. Reinforce to him that delegation does not mean abdication. Breaking a complex project into manageable chunks, each with clearly defined milestones, makes effective follow-up easier. It's also important to schedule regular meetings before the project even begins in order to ensure that the manager stays abreast of progress and that staff members feel accountable.

Getting Support from Above

Most first-time managers see their relationship with their boss more as one of servitude than of partnership.

They will wait for you to initiate meetings, ask for reports, and question results. You may welcome this restraint, but generally it's a bad sign. For one thing, it puts undue pressure on you to keep the flow of communication going. Even more important, it prevents new managers from looking to you as a critical source of support. If they don't see you that way, it's unlikely that they will see themselves that way for their own people. The problem isn't only that your position intimidates them; it's also that they fear being vulnerable. A newly promoted manager doesn't want you to see weaknesses, lest you think you made a mistake in promoting her. When I ask rookie managers about their relationships with their bosses, they often admit that they are trying to "stay under the boss's radar" and are "careful about what [they] say to the boss."

Some inexperienced managers will not seek your help even when they start to founder. Seemingly capable rookie managers often try to cover up a failing project or relationship—just until they can get it back under control. For example, one manager I worked with at a technology company hired a professional 20 years her senior. The transition was rocky, and, despite her best efforts, the individual wasn't acclimating to the organization. (The company, like many in the technology sector, was very youth oriented.) Rather than reaching out to her boss for help, the manager continued to grapple with the situation alone. The staff member ultimately resigned at the busiest time of the year, and the young manager suffered the dual punishment of being understaffed at the worst possible moment and having it known that she had lost a potentially important contributor.

What's the boss of a rookie manager to do? You can begin by clarifying expectations. Explain the connection between the rookie's success and your success, so that she understands that open communication is necessary for you to achieve your goals. Explain that you don't expect her to have all the answers. Introduce her to other managers within the company who may be helpful, and encourage her to contact them as needed. Let her know that mistakes happen but that the cover-up is always worse than the crime. Let her know that you like to receive occasional lunch invitations as much as you like to extend them.

Lunch and drop-by meetings are important, but they usually aren't enough. Consider meeting regularly with a new manager—perhaps weekly in the early stages of a new assignment, moving to biweekly or monthly as her confidence builds. These meetings will develop rapport, provide you with insight into how the person is approaching the job, and make the new manager organize her thoughts on a regular basis. Be clear that the meetings are her time and that it's up to her to plan the agenda. You're there to ask and answer questions and to offer advice. The message you send is that the individual's work is important to you and that you're a committed business partner. More subtly, you're modeling how to simultaneously empower and guide direct reports.

Projecting Confidence

Looking confident when you don't feel confident—it's a challenge we all face, and as senior managers we're usually conscious of the need when it arises. Rookie managers are often so internally focused that they are unaware of this need or the image they project. They are so focused on substance that they forget that form counts, too. The first weeks and months on the job are a critical time for new leaders to reach out to staff. If they don't project confidence, they are unlikely to inspire and energize their teams.

I routinely work with new managers who are unaware that their everyday demeanor is hurting their organizations. In one rapidly growing technology company, the service manager, Linda, faced high levels of stress. Service outages were all too common, and they were beyond her control. Customers were exacting, and they too were under great pressure. Her rapidly growing staff was generally inexperienced. Distraught customers and employees had her tied up in knots almost daily. She consistently appeared breathless, rushed, and fearful that the other shoe was about to drop. The challenge was perhaps too big for a first-time manager, but that's what happens in rapidly growing companies. On one level, Linda was doing an excellent job keeping the operation going. The client base was growing and retention was certainly high—largely as a result of her energy and resourcefulness. But on another level, she was doing a lot of damage.

Linda's frantic demeanor had two critical repercussions. First, she had unwittingly defined the standard for acceptable conduct in her department, and her inexperienced staff began to display the same behaviors. Before long, other departments were reluctant to communicate with Linda or her team, for fear of bothering them or eliciting an emotional reaction. But for the company to arrive at real solutions to the service problems, departments needed to openly exchange information, and that wasn't happening. Second, Linda was not portraying herself to senior managers as promotion material. They were pleased with her troubleshooting abilities, but they did not see a confident, thoughtful senior manager in the making. The image

Linda was projecting would ultimately hold back both her career and her department.

Not all rookie managers display the problems that Linda did. Some appear excessively arrogant. Others wear their self-doubt on their sleeves. Whether your managers appear overwhelmed, arrogant, or insecure, honest feedback is your best tool. You can help rookie managers by telling them that it's always safe to let out their feelings—in your office, behind closed doors. Reinforce just how long a shadow they cast once they assume leadership positions. Their staff members watch them closely, and if they see professionalism and optimism, they are likely to demonstrate those characteristics as well. Preach the gospel of conscious comportment—a constant awareness of the image one is projecting to the world. If you observe a manager projecting a less-than-positive image, tell that person right away.

You should also be alert to new managers who undermine their own authority. Linda made another classic rookie mistake when she attempted to get her staff members to implement an initiative that her boss had come up with. In presenting the initiative, she let her team know it was important to implement because it had come from the division's senior vice president. While her intentions were good—rallying the team to perform—her words encouraged the group to focus attention above her rather than on her. There is no quicker way for a rookie manager to lose credibility with her staff than to appear to be a mouthpiece for senior management. Pointing out that senior management will be checking up on the initiative certainly won't hurt, but the rookie manager must take care never to be perceived simply as the messenger.

Just-in-time coaching is often the most effective method for showing rookie managers how to project confidence. For instance, the first time you ask a new manager to carry out an initiative, take a little extra time to walk her through the process. Impress upon her the cardinal rule of management: Your staff members don't necessarily have to like you, but they do need to trust you. Ensure that the new manager owns the message she's delivering.

Rookie managers have a real knack for allowing immediate tasks to overshadow overarching initiatives.

Layoffs are a classic example of a message the rookie manager will struggle with. Don't allow a rookie to proceed half-prepared. Share as much information as you can. Make sure she's ready for all the likely questions and reactions by asking her to do an informal dry run with you. You might be surprised by how poorly she conveys the message in her first few attempts. A little practice may preserve the image of your manager and your company.

Focusing on the Big Picture

Rookie managers have a real knack for allowing immediate tasks to overshadow overarching initiatives. This is particularly true for those promoted from within, because they've just come from the front lines where they're accustomed to constant fire fighting. As a recent individual contributor armed with plenty of technical know-how, the rookie manager instinctively runs to the immediate rescue of any client or staff member in need. The sense of accomplishment rookies get from such rescues is seductive and far more exhilarating than rooting out the cause of all the fire fighting. And what could be better for team spirit than having the boss jump into the trenches and fight the good fight?

Of course, a leader shows great team spirit if he joins the troops in emergencies. But are all those emergencies true emergencies? Are newer staff members being empowered to handle complex challenges? And if the rookie manager is busy fighting fires, who is thinking strategically for the department? If you're the senior manager and these questions are popping into your head, you may well have a rookie manager who doesn't fully understand his role or is afraid to seize it.

I recently worked with a young manager who had become so accustomed to responding to a steady flow of problems that he was reluctant to block off any time to work on the strategic initiatives we had identified. When I probed, he revealed that he felt a critical part of his role was to wait for crises to arise. "What if I schedule this time and something urgent comes up and I disappoint someone?" he asked. When I pointed out that he could always postpone his strategy sessions if a true emergency arose, he seemed relieved. But he saw the concept of making time to think about the business as self-indulgent—this, despite the fact that his group was going to be asked to raise productivity significantly in the following fiscal year, and he'd done nothing to prepare for that reality.

Senior managers can help rookies by explaining to them that strategic thinking is a necessary skill for career advancement: For first-time managers, 10% of the work might be strategic and 90% tactical. As executives climb the corporate ladder, however, those percentages will flip-flop. To be successful at the next level, managers must demonstrate that they can think and act strategically. You can use your regularly scheduled meetings to help your managers focus on the big picture. Don't allow them to simply review the latest results and move on. Ask probing questions about those results. For example, "What trends are you seeing in the marketplace that could affect you in two quarters? Tell me how your competition is responding to those same trends." Don't let them regale you with the wonderful training their staffs have been getting without asking, "What additional skills do we need to build in the staff to increase productivity by 25% next year?" If you aren't satisfied with your managers' responses, let them know that you expect them to think this way—not to have all the answers, but to be fully engaged in the strategic thought process.

Rookie managers commonly focus on activities rather than on goals. That's because activities can be accomplished quickly (for example, conducting a seminar to improve the sales staff's presentation skills), whereas achieving goals generally takes more time (for example, actually enhancing the sales staff's effectiveness). The senior manager can help the rookie manager think strategically by asking for written goals that clearly distinguish between the goals and their supporting activities. Insisting on a goal-setting discipline will help your new (and not-so-new) managers to organize their strategic game plans. Critical but soft goals, such as staff development, are often overlooked because they are difficult to measure. Putting such goals in print with clear action steps makes them concrete, rendering a sense of accomplishment when they are achieved and a greater likelihood that they will be rewarded. Managers with clear goals will be less tempted to become full-time tacticians. Just as important, the process will help you ensure that they are thinking about the right issues and deploying their teams effectively.

Giving Constructive Feedback

It's human nature to avoid confrontations, and most
people feel awkward when they have to correct others'
behavior or actions. Rookie managers are no exception,
and they often avoid addressing important issues with
their staff. The typical scenario goes something like this:
A staff member is struggling to meet performance goals
or is acting inappropriately in meetings. The manager
sits back, watches, and hopes that things will magically
improve. Other staff members observe the situation and
become frustrated by the manager's inaction. The manager's own frustration builds, as she can't believe the
subordinate doesn't get it. The straightforward performance issue has now evolved into a credibility problem.
When the manager finally addresses the problem, she
personalizes it, lets her frustration seep into the discussion with her staff member, and finds the recipient rush-
ing to defend himself from attack.

Most inexperienced managers wait far too long to talk
with staff about performance problems. The senior manager can help by creating an environment in which constructive feedback is perceived not as criticism but as a
source of empowerment. This begins with the feedback
you offer to your managers about their own development. It can be as simple as getting them to tell you
where their weaknesses are before they become problem-
atic. After a good performance review, for example, you
might say to your new manager, "By all accounts, you
have a bright future here, so it's important that we talk
about what you *don't* want me to know. What are you
feeling least confident about? How can we address those
areas so that you're ready for any opportunity that
arises?" You'll probably be surprised by how attuned
most high performers are to their own development

needs. But they are not likely to do much about them unless you put those needs on the table.

More than likely, the feedback your managers have to offer their staffs will not always be so positive or easy to deliver. The key is to foster in them the desire to help their reports achieve their goals. Under those circumstances, even loathsome personal issues become approachable.

One of my clients managed a high-performing senior staff member who was notably unhelpful to others in the department and who resented her own lack of advancement. Instead of avoiding the issue because he didn't want to tell the staff member that she had a bad attitude, the senior manager took a more productive approach. He leveraged his knowledge of her personal goals to introduce the feedback. "I know that you're anxious for your first management role, and one of my goals is to help you attain that. I can't do that unless I'm completely honest with you. A big part of management is developing stronger skills in your staff. You aren't demonstrating that you enjoy that role. How can we can work together on that?" No guilt, no admonishment—just an offer to help her get what she wanted. Yet the message was received loud and clear.

A brainstorming session this client and I had about ways to offer critical feedback led to that approach. Often, brainstorming sessions can help rookie managers see that sticky personal issues can be broken down into straightforward business issues. In the case of the unhelpful senior staff member, her attitude didn't really need to enter the discussion; her actions did. Recommending a change in action is much easier than recommending a change in attitude. Never forget the old saw: You can't ask people to change their personalities, but you can ask them to change their behaviors.

Indeed, senior managers should share their own techniques for dealing with difficult conversations. One manager I worked with became defensive whenever a staff member questioned her judgment. She didn't really need me to tell her that her behavior was undermining her image and effectiveness. She did need me to offer her some techniques that would enable her to respond differently in the heat of the moment. She trained herself to respond quickly and earnestly with a small repertoire of questions like, "Can you tell me more about what you mean by that?" This simple technique bought her the time she needed to gather her thoughts and engage in an interchange that was productive rather than defensive. She was too close to the situation to come up with the technique herself.

Delegating, thinking strategically, communicating—you may think this all sounds like Management 101. And you're right. The most basic elements of management are often what trip up managers early in their careers. And because they are the basics, the bosses of rookie managers often take them for granted. They shouldn't—an extraordinary number of people fail to develop these skills. I've maintained an illusion throughout this article—that only rookie managers suffer because they haven't mastered these core skills. But the truth is, managers at all levels make these mistakes. An organization that supports its new managers by helping them to develop these skills will have surprising advantages over the competition.

Originally published in April 2002
Reprint R0204H

About the Contributors

RONALD N. ASHKENAS is a Managing Partner of Robert H. Schaffer & Associates and an internationally recognized consultant, executive coach, and speaker on organizational transformation. His clients have included Fortune 500 firms, government agencies, The Federal Reserve Bank of New York, the World Bank, and many other large and medium-sized companies. In addition, Ron was one of the lead consultants for General Electric's "Work-Out" process, and helped to develop GE Capital's approach to acquisition integration. Ron holds a master's degree from Harvard University and a doctorate in organizational behavior from Case Western Reserve University.

DR. STEVEN BERGLAS is a management consultant and executive coach who spent twenty-five years on the faculty of Harvard Medical School's Department of Psychiatry and had a private psychotherapy practice in Boston prior to relocating to Los Angeles in 1999. Dr. Berglas's professional practice involves consulting to businesses on the factors that maximize the quality of executives' decision making, training managers and senior executives to prevent career burnout, and coaching executives who have engaged in self-defeating behavior. Berglas's academic research focuses on identifying the psychological factors that motivate entrepreneurial success and how corporate executives can learn to function in an entrepreneurial manner. He also designs and implements programs for banking and investment institutions to prevent white-collar crime.

DR. HEIKE BRUCH is a professor and Director at the Institute for Leadership and Human Resources Management of the University of St. Gallen (Switzerland). She got her Ph.D. from the University of Hanover (1996) and her master's (1991) and bachelor's degrees (1989) in Business Administration from the Free University of Berlin. Bruch's research is strongly focused on leadership. She works in close cooperation with international universities both in research and teaching, where she focuses on managers' emotion, volition, and action as well as leadership in change processes and organizational energy. She has written four books, edited six, and published more than forty articles in journals and books.

HARRIS COLLINGWOOD is a former Harvard Business Review senior editor who writes frequently on leadership, business, and finance. His articles include "The Earnings Game: Everyone Plays, Nobody Wins," published in the June 2001 issue of the *Harvard Business Review*. He lives in Cambridge, MA.

SUMANTRA GHOSHAL is Professor of Strategic and International Management at the London Business School. His research focuses on strategic, organizational, and managerial issues confronting large, global companies. He has published eleven books, over seventy articles, and several award-winning case studies, including *Managing Across Borders: The Transnational Solution*, a book he coauthored with Christopher Bartlett. With doctoral degrees from both the MIT Sloan School of Management and the Harvard Business School, Sumantra serves on the editorial boards of several academic journals and has been nominated to the Fellowships at the Academy of Management, the Academy of International Business, and the World Economic Forum.

JULIA KIRBY is a senior editor at the *Harvard Business Review*, where she develops articles on a wide range of management topics. She also manages the magazine's case study section, in which common managerial dilemmas are presented in fictional form.

JOHN P. KOTTER is a graduate of MIT and Harvard. He is the author of six books that have won awards or honors and seven that have been business best-sellers. In October 2001, *BusinessWeek* magazine reported a survey they conducted of 504 enterprises that rated Professor Kotter the number-one leadership guru in America. He lives in Cambridge, Massachusetts, and in Ashland, New Hampshire, with his wife, Nancy Dearman, daughter, Caroline, and son, Jonathan.

JIM LOEHR, a performance psychologist, has worked with hundreds of professional athletes, including Monica Seles, Dan Jansen, and Mark O'Meara. Loehr is also a cofounder and the CEO of LGE Performance Systems in Orlando, Florida, a consulting firm that applies training principals developed in sports to business executives. Dr. Loehr has authored twelve books, which have been translated into a half-dozen languages, including recent best-seller *Stress for Success* (Times Books). Dr. Loehr holds a master's and doctorate degree in counseling psychology from the University of Northern Colorado.

WILLIAM ONCKEN, JR., founded his company, the William Oncken Corporation, in 1960 in New York City. He set as his mission to provide management development programs deeply rooted in the realities of the management environment. He conveyed the philosophies he created by using his own unique vocabulary and imagery.

ROBERT H. SCHAFFER is a principal in Robert H. Schaffer & Associates, the Stamford, Connecticut, management consulting firm. He is the author of over fifty articles on management and on consulting and has served as Editor of the *Journal of Management Consulting*. His book *High-Impact Consulting: How Clients and Consultants Can Work Together to Achieve Extraordinary Results* was published by Jossey-Bass in 2002. The book focuses on how to close the "implementation gap" that so often exists between the advice given and the actual change a client makes.

TONY SCHWARTZ is President of LGE Performance and the author of *What Really Matters: Searching for Wisdom in America* (Bantam, 1996) and *Work In Progress* with Michael Eisner (Random House, 1998). Schwartz is coauthor with Jim Loehr of the upcoming *The Power of Full Engagement* (Simon and Schuster, January 2003).

CAROL A. WALKER is the President of Prepared to Lead, a consulting firm devoted to helping organizations maximize the effectiveness of first-time managers. Ms. Walker specializes in customized one-on-one coaching, focusing on objectives established mutually between the individual and the employer. Prior to founding Prepared to Lead, Ms. Walker spent fourteen years in the Northeast Regional office of the Chubb Corporation, where she managed global property and casualty operations. Later, she served as a Senior Vice President for CCBN, a leading provider of Internet-based communications for corporate investor relations. Ms. Walker holds an M.B.A. from the Simmons Graduate School of Management and a B.A. in Sociology from Dartmouth College.

DONALD L. WASS, PH.D., was President of the William Oncken Company of Texas when this article first appeared. He now heads the Dallas-Fort Worth Region of The Executive Committee (TEC), an international organization for presidents and CEOs.

Index

intimacy, fear of, 138–139
IPS. *See* Ideal Performance
  State

job requirements
  behaviors of general man-
    agers and, 53–54
  dealing with subordinates
    and, 95–96
  demands for performance
    improvement and, 95–96
  nonmanagerial tasks and,
    94–95, 157–159
  sources of anxiety in, 94–98
  strategies for anxiety reduc-
    tion and, 98–106
Jones, Marion, 77
journal writing, 86
just-in-time coaching, 157

Karl, Klaus, 35–37
Kinder, Joe, 120

leadership. *See also* senior
    management
  empowerment and, 13–16
  executive interest in, 109,
    110–111
  followers and, 112, 114, 117,
    121–125
  handling of crises and,
    125–127
  important tasks of leaders
    and, 111–114
  projection of confidence
    and, 154–157
  roundtable on, 109–128

value added and, 112,
    113–114, 117–121
  vision and, 111, 113, 114–117
"learned helplessness," 23–24
LG Electronics, 19
Lufthansa, 19, 20–21, 23,
    24–25, 27, 28–29, 33

management time, 1–16. *See
    also* time management
  elimination of subordinate-
    imposed time and, 8–11
  empowerment and, 13–16
  managerial rules and, 11–12
  monkey-on-the-back
    metaphor and, 3–12
  origin of subordinate-
    imposed time and, 3–8
  types of, 2–3
management training pro-
    grams, 59
managerial behavior. *See* focus-
    energy matrix
Maslow, Abraham, 14, 140
McBride, Glenn, 124
McGuire, Mike, 126
meditation, 81, 86
mental capacity, 71, 80–84
Merck, 114–115, 116–117, 119,
    125
Mintzberg, Henry, 46, 106
monkey-on-the-back
    metaphor, 3–12
  elimination of subordinate-
    imposed time and, 8–11
  empowerment and, 13–16
  managerial rules and, 11–12